The pictures brought the scriptures to reality for our present time. (1Peter 1:19-20) "But with the precious blood of Christ, as of a lamb without blemish and without spot: What a miraculous blessing for the Lord to show up on the cover of my book. I felt that it was a stamp of God's approval to my life story and testimony of the Lord Jesus Christ coming into my life and dying for my sins. As well as, rescuing me from all of the strong holds upon my life. I believe that God wants everyone to hear his voice and know the truth of Jesus Christ coming into the world and dying on the cross for the sins of the whole world. That who so ever believe, on him should not parish but have eternal life.

Both front and back covers have a tint added to it, to help reveal the supernatural images.

Picture #1

About The Cover

When I began writing this book, I had a particular vision that I wanted the front cover to represent and express to its viewers. The vision was to match the title of the book as well as, represent the deliverance upon my life story without words. I wanted the picture to portray my life being delivered from the past lifestyle of "Homosexuality," to my new lifestyle of complete "Holiness," while honoring God with my body.

The pictures were taken in my apartment, in front of my fire place, located in Indianapolis, Indiana in the month of June 2014. I had a very close friend there with me, to represent the enemy in the picture. He was standing behind a tall pole that had white sheets on it, with broken chains in his hands, while wearing a mask. The white sheets, represents the surrendering to the purifying of my life. The broken chains in his hands represented the homosexual lifestyle that no longer had me bound. I was on the other side of the pole squatting down, looking up and reverencing God for delivering me from the hands of the enemy. I had on my "Tallit" or prayer shawl, that revealed God's covering and his power upon my life as well as his grace and mercy.

The picture was taken with my "LG Flex" cell phone that was set on a timer and programed on shutter. In which shutter means, it takes multiple shots over a very small period of time. There was fire blazing in the fire place and broken chain pieces on the floor, to add to the scenery. After we took a couple of shots I looked at the pictures and to my surprise, there were four photos that had images in them that were not a part of the scenery. In the first three pictures I noticed there were images that appeared in the fire of the fire place that I did not know exactly what they were. The next picture had taken my breath away. There was an image of a cross with a body in front of it between me and the guy that represented the enemy. I instantly knew who and what this was about, upon first sight. It was Jesus Christ! His head was transparent to the images in the fire but it was still on his body outside of the fire. The Holy Spirit then told me that Jesus appeared here on the cross, to represent the defeating of the enemy for me and delivering me from sin. God would later reveal to me the images in the fire, which is one of the creatures, from (Ezekiel 1:10) with the four faces. They four had the face of a man and the face of a lion on the right side, they had the face of an ox on the left side and they also had the face of an eagle. The body even reflected the wings that were described in the scriptures.

Ezekiel (1:4-28) And I looked, and, behold, a whirlwind came out of the north, a great cloud, and a fire infolding itself, and a brightness was about it, and out of the midst thereof as the color of amber, out of the midst of the fire. 5 Also out of the midst there of came the likeness of four living creatures. And this was their appearance; they had the likeness of a man. 6 And every one had four faces, and every one had four wings. 7 And their feet were straight feet; and the sole of their feet was like the sole of a calf's foot: and they sparkled like the color of burnished brass. 8 And they had the hands of a man under their wings on their four sides; and they four had their faces and their wings. 9 Their wings were joined one to another; they turned not when they went; they went every one straight forward. 10 As for the likeness of their faces, they four had the face of a man, and the face of a lion, on the right side: and they four had the face of an ox on the left side; they four also had the face of an eagle. 11 Thus were their faces: and their wings were stretched upward; two wings of every one were joined one to another, and two covered their bodies. 12 And they went every one straight forward: whither the spirit was to go, they went; and they turned not when they went. 13 As for the likeness of the living creatures, their appearance was like burning coals of fire, and like the appearance of lamps: it went up and down among the living creatures; and the fire was bright, and out of the fire went forth lightning. 14 And the living creatures ran and returned as the appearance of a flash of lightning.

15 Now as I beheld the living creatures, behold one wheel upon the earth by the living creatures, with his four faces. 16 The appearance of the wheels and their work was like unto the color of a beryl: and they four had one likeness: and their appearance and their work was as it were a wheel in the middle of a wheel. 17 When they went, they went upon their four sides: and they turned not when they went. 18 As for their rings, they were so high that they were dreadful; and their rings were full of eyes round about them four. 19 And when the living creatures went, the wheels went by them: and when the living creatures were lifted up from the earth, the wheels were lifted up. 20 Whithersoever the spirit was to go, they went, thither was their spirit to go; and the wheels were lifted up over against them: for the spirit of the living

creature was in the wheels. 21 When those went, these went; and when those stood, these stood; and when those were lifted up from the earth, the wheels were lifted up over against them: for the spirit of the living creature was in the wheels. 22 And the likeness of the firmament upon the heads of the living creature was as the color of the terrible crystal, stretched forth over their heads above. 23 And under the firmament were their wings straight, the one toward the other: everyone had two, which covered on this side, and every one had two, which covered on that side, their bodies. 24 And when they went, I heard the noise of their wings, like the noise of great waters, as the voice of the Almighty, the voice of speech, as the noise of an host: when they stood, they let down their wings. 25 And there was a voice from the firmament that was over their heads, when they stood, and had let down their wings.

    26 And above the firmament that was over their heads was the likeness of a throne, as the appearance of a sapphire stone: and upon the likeness of the throne was the likeness as the appearance of a man above upon it. 27 And I saw as the color of amber, as the appearance of fire round about within it, from the appearance of his loins even upward, and from the appearance of his loins even downward, I saw as it were the appearance of fire, and it had brightness round about. 28 As the appearance of the bow that is in the cloud in the day of rain, so was the appearance of the brightness round about. This was the appearance of the likeness of the glory of the Lord.

Picture #2

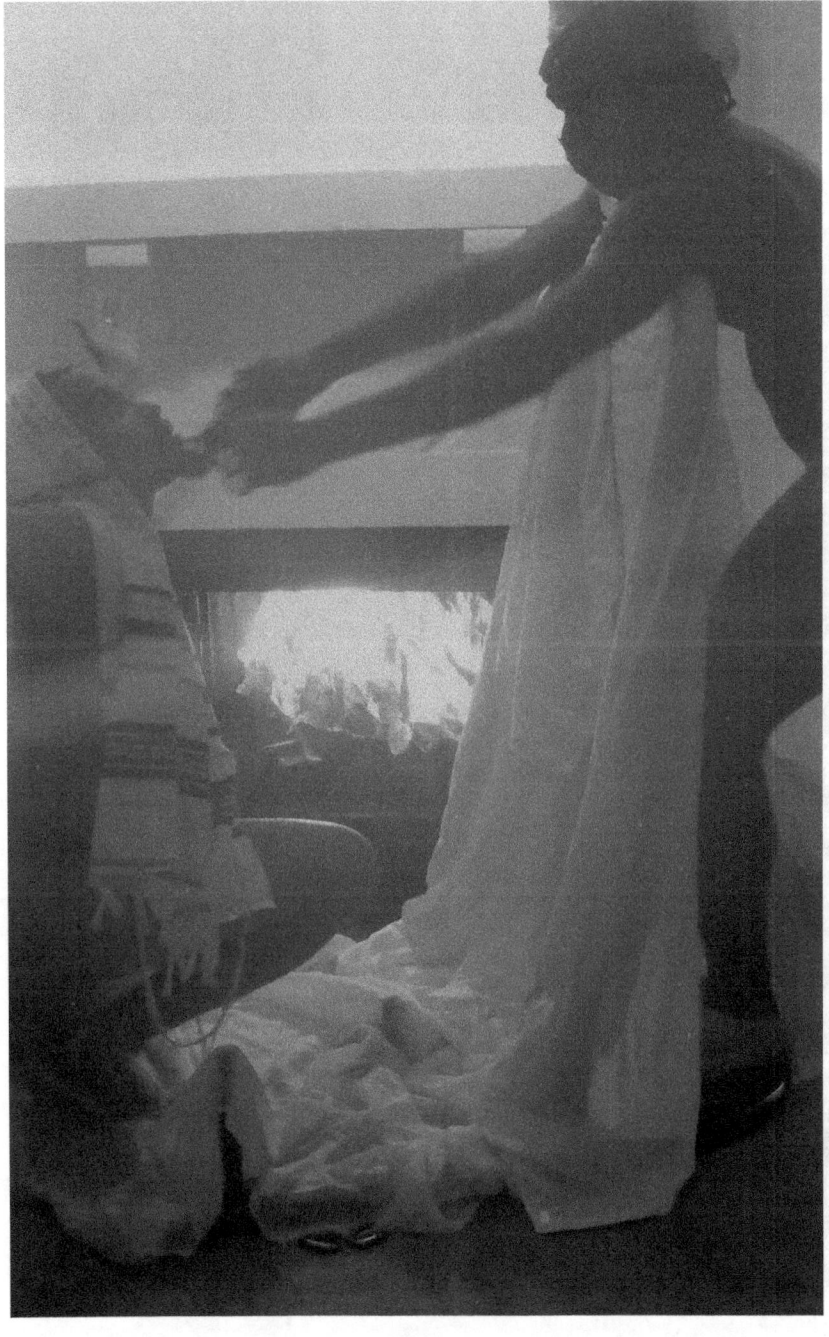

Picture #3

Picture #4

The Totality OF Deliverance

Get Ready For Your Life Is About To Change!

By Apostle Antwan Amey

Totality Of Deliverance Copyright © 2014 by Antwan Amey.

All rights reserved. Printed in the United States of America. No part of this book may be used or reproduced in any manner what so ever without written permission.

Scripture quotations were taken from the New International, King James version.

For information contact; address www.ameyantwan@yahoo.com

Book and Cover design by Antwan Amey

ISBN: 13 :978-0692360514

ISBN : 10 :0692360514

CONTENTS

CONTENTS XII

PROLOGUE 1

THE LIFE OF ANTWAN AMEY

PART 1- Adolescent……………………….......4

PART 2- Late Teens/Early Twenties…………....19

PART 3- Late Twenties……………………...50

PART 4- Early Thirties………………….....67

THE PHASES OF DELIVERANCE

1. Deliverance………………………………...85

2. Freedom……………………………………88

3. Darken Heart...……………..……………94

4. Vile Passions…………………………….96

5. Reprobate Mind……………………….101

6. The Process……………………………….105

7. Praise and Worship……………………109

8. Spiritually Walking……………………….113

9. Power From On High..............................117

10. Perseverance..120

11. Set Free...124

12. Your New Character............................129

My Outlook On Total Deliverance.................133

Acknowledgements....................................139

About the Author.......................................141

About the Editor.......................................143

But rise, and stand upon thy feet:

for I have appeared unto thee for this purpose,

to make thee a minister and a witness

both of these things which thou hast seen,

and of those things in the which I will appear unto thee;

Delivering thee from the people,

and from the Gentiles,

unto whom now I send thee,

To open their eyes, and to

Turn them from darkness to light,

and from the power of Satan unto God,

that they may receive forgiveness of sins,

and inheritance among them which

are sanctified by faith that is in me.

(Acts 26:16-18)

Prologue

For me, I felt the alternative lifestyle come over me at the early age of five. I began to understand that I was different or something was different about me even from the beginning of my school years as well. I can remember a time in kindergarten, when we had to form our daily circle and play the "Word Learning Game." We had to hold hands in this circle with other class mates. I noticed that there was a really handsome boy that caught my eye and all of my attention. My mind instantly thought, "Ummm I know whose hand, I'm going to hold!" As I ran over to hold his hand, this pretty little girl with two ponytails in her hair, by the name of Brittany had jumped in between us. I tried my best to push her away to hold somebody else's hand, but she was so anxious and persistent to hold his hand. Although, he had two hands I did not want her to hold neither one of them. I was irritated as I watched how much she had adored him, and how fast she came from the opposite side of the circle, just to hold his hand. I then began to fight her by first pinching her; she looked at me and said "ooocheee" that hurt. Next, I immediately bit her on the arm extremely hard. I had tried everything and anything that I could, to keep her very far away from him or should I say us. She then stood in the center of the circle pouting, crying and pointing into the area where I was standing, but the teacher grabbed her and held her

THE TOTALITY OF DELIVERANCE

hand. I did not care about her telling on me as long as she held somebody else's hand I would be ok. Of course I held his hand and it felt so good that I thought to myself, "I am going to hold his hand every day." The feeling that I had while I was holding his hand was unexplainable, but I loved and enjoyed every moment of it. When I got home from school this incident was brought back to my memory. Once I had thought about it, I realized that she was right and that I was completely wrong. It was the Holy Spirit that came over me, and helped me to realize in full details, why I was wrong. However, this was an event that I would remember for a lifetime because, I knew that boys were created to like girls, but for me I liked the boys.

THE TOTALITY OF DELIVERANCE

THE LIFE

OF

ANTWAN AMEY

Part 1

(Adolescent)

Darken Heart ~ Vile Passions

At an early age I had known that there was something different about me. I began to feel like the black sheep, and not just of my family but my friends too. I felt, as if I was a totally different being, because I did not like what the normal boys would like to do for fun. Football, basketball, climbing trees, fighting and just things that males would do around the neighborhood I did not enjoy. I would rather be in the house with the females of the family doing hair, dressing up in dresses, pumps, women church hats, playing with Barbies, baby dolls, and cooking with my grandmother Luvenia Kilpatrick (MA), who I loved so dear. We enjoyed each others company no matter what we were doing. She made me feel like I was normal and special to her. Then there was my grandfather Jim Kilpatrick, who was my best friend. He would always instruct me on the things that were to come in the later days of my life with his wisdom, which was given whenever we had gone fishing together or any alone time.

THE TOTALITY OF DELIVERANCE

He also made me feel special and well-loved whenever we were around each other. When it came to being around both of my grandparents at the same time, there was nowhere else that I would even desire to be. To me my grandparent's house was the best place on earth. Then there was my mom Janice Smith, (BaBa) she was an immediate answer to my total life situation. She is a woman of integrity, that is very understanding, and so much wisdom when it came to the things that she did and believed in. Nevertheless she made very smart choices, when it came to those things that she did not know. I was the first born of the three children my mother had and the two step children that were added to the family by my mom's, marriage at a very early age. Even with the two outsiders added to the family, I still felt like an outcast. I received much love from the entire family, in which had a very exclusive number of three hundred or more. While I was still young the family was still growing and had increased to six large generations of family members. Then there was my sister Germany who is two years younger than me. She was a very pretty girl that I do love dearly. We were always pretty close but as she had gotten older she started to live out her name. It would be safe to say that her actions started saying "Nazi" as she began her early teenage years. She took no stuff off of anyone and would fight at the drop of a dime in school or out of school

THE TOTALITY OF DELIVERANCE

and was always in some type of trouble. It could have come from our home life or it could have been from the spirit behind her name, however her name described her to a "T". Then there was my younger brother Aarun who is four years younger than I. He was extremely spoiled and did not know it. We were pretty close as well, although he did not take on the Nazi action like my sister, he still was different in his own way but he rarely got into any major trouble, like Germany. Next, there was Todd my stepfather who was ok when I was younger except the time when my grandmother had bought me a baby doll and he took the doll and told me that boys don't play with dolls. I immediately bust out of the door and ran down the street, crying to my grandmother's house to tell her. In which she came to our house and told him to give me my doll back and whatever I was going to be when I grew up, didn't have anything to do with him. As I began to get older, our relationship became very distant. He did teach me how to do something's like working on cars because he was really good in those days with cars and playing board games etc. After all he was my mother's husband but I must admit he was not one of my favorite people to be around at that time. I can remember a time, when I was younger and my mom sent him to come and pick me up from my grandparent's house, when I just shook my head saying, "nope, nope, nope," the whole time he was

THE TOTALITY OF DELIVERANCE

telling me to come on lets go. He called my mom and she told him that it was ok, to leave me there. I didn't like to be around him mainly because, he was very argumentative and always fussing when it came to any of us who lived under the same roof as him. Also, he didn't mind whooping us for any small or big thing that he didn't like.

My father (Eric Amey) was really not in the picture. He lived in another state, but I really had no contact with him until I was about twelve years of age. He moved back to Indiana and told me that he had come back home to help take care of me, and that he was going to be a father to me to make up for all of the years that he had missed. It was then I could find the comfort of having a father and a mother that really cared for me and could help answer some of the questions that was roaming around my heart, about my life and my sexuality. He was around for those summer months, Thanksgiving, Christmas and my birthday, man that really meant the world to me! As I sit back and think about the days that we spent together; that little bit of time when he was around, really did create a lifetime of memories for me. Within nine months of him being home and becoming the father that I had needed and longed for, he was then murdered. I had lost my father to gambling, a game of dice.

THE TOTALITY OF DELIVERANCE

Now, I'm back to the drawing board of not having what I felt was missing for years. During this time I begin to remember all of the things that the preacher would talk about while we were at church. The preacher would talk about how God is a father to you and how he would never leave you and will always be there when there was no one else. As a child and up to my teenage years my grandfather was the superintendent for the church that our family attended and belonged to. It was a Baptist church not too far from our home. Every Sunday morning I would go with my grandfather to unlock the doors of the church and sit on the front row, while eating peppermints and sleeping until the rest of the congregation arrived. Most of the time, it would be my cousins, my sister, my brother, me, and anyone else who spent a night over my grandparent's house on Saturday nights. I was listening and I did hear the sermons, but it really didn't mean much at that time, so I thought. I guess it was sinking into my mind and my heart because, I then remembered that I needed the God that the preacher was always preaching about, when my father got murdered. It didn't stop my success at school, because I was an honor student and yet willing to pursue my dreams of becoming a Preacher, Teacher, Doctor, and Hair stylist, but it did add to the burden of my heart. That is the hope of one day having a father that I could call and he would be there for me, if

THE TOTALITY OF DELIVERANCE

nothing else but for support. I felt the separation of my life coming between me and my stepfather. I believed it was my choice of lifestyle and the differences of his family beliefs and my mother's family beliefs.

As I grew older, I can still remember trying to fit in with the rest of the gentlemen but it just did not work for me. I tried everything in my will power to do the things that most young men would do, but still it was just not happening for me. I then began to feel the separation at school too. I felt the need to make sure that at the very least I had dressed accordingly to the fashion of young men at that time. Being, that we were not as wealthy as most other families, I felt the need to go and get my own job at the age of fourteen. Mainly, because that was the age when my mom had gone school shopping for me, and she came home with some cheap "LA Gears" tennis shoes. I made myself a promise that this would never happen to me again. So, I immediately had my grandmother to take me job hunting, and it was very successful. I begin working my first job that next week and was extremely excited because it was a banquet and catering job for the "Indy 500 Racing Inn". I made a pretty amount of money there plus the staff and my boss loved me so much, sometimes we would all spend a night at that place; on the weekends just to laugh and be around each other. It was helping out but not like I desired. So, I began working two jobs with

THE TOTALITY OF DELIVERANCE

the second job being a pizza restaurant, while going to school at the same time. All the while, I was still keeping my honor roll status and marvelous grades. In fact this was the year that I was inducted into the "Who's Who Among American Students Book." Being, the separation that I had felt in myself and society, I felt as if I needed my own transportation to accelerate my personal needs and goals. Not to mention, I hated riding the school bus with those other kids, it was just not my style. Also, I did not have the patience to ride on that bus, going from stop to stop with my stop always being last. So, I enrolled myself into Drivers Ed and began to work towards my driver license and getting my own automobile. It was a success! With this happening, it helped me to get to the next level of my life, in which I was a firm believer in God our Savior the Lord Jesus Christ would help me every step along the way. I stayed at church and sung in the choir and the school's gospel choir, the majority of time in my youth and school years. Not to mention that my stepfather's family had a gospel choir that I sung with also.

    I was always praying, praising and giving God the glory but yet, I did not have the right outlook on life, the outlook that God wanted me to have. I would pray for things and the way that I wanted them to turn out. Mostly, because I felt God would answer every prayer that I prayed, in which my life would always reveal and reflect

THE TOTALITY OF DELIVERANCE

that God was somewhere working in the midst of it. I would always notice that there were small voices that were in my ear, whenever I was about to make a decision, any choice or just sitting around thinking about my life. One voice would suggest that I would do things the wrong way or tell me to do things that I knew were not right. On the other hand, the other voice would tell me to do the right things and also tell me the outcome of the situation, if I were to live the right way and make the good choices in my life. The voices became very familiar because I consistently heard them at a very early age.

Then all of a sudden things went up in an uproar at home, my stepfather and I could not get along for nothing in the world. I then began to break down and was sick of this lifestyle that had begun to take place in my life. I was tired of my home life, work, school and feeling like a misfit to the family and to this whole world. I felt, as if I needed to be secluded from everything and everyone but I could not find a way out. The living arrangements started to really get to me the most, out of everything that had begun to bother me. My younger brother Aarun and I shared bedrooms and when my stepbrother Vernon came over it was a very tight fit, until I got totally fed up with this arrangement, when I was just about the age of sixteen. That's when I saved up my money and then paid for a bedroom to be built in our basement to be far away

THE TOTALITY OF DELIVERANCE

from everyone. Finally, I got to have a safe haven of my own. The room, did began a new chapter in my life, in which I began to be the person that I was led to be in my mind and in my heart. I had become adapted to having my own living arrangements that did prepare me for my own home. I then added my own phone line, at that time cell phones were not quit established yet, so it was the means to contact my friends, besides beepers. In which, my friends were others who shared similar lifestyles like the lifestyle that I chose to live in. I believe it was part of the coming out proportion of the homosexual lifestyle, that I had been dealing with inside. I had a really good friend that we did almost everything together, being we had gone to the same school, worked our own job and had our own vehicles. We first started creeping out downtown to a gay bar that was twenty-one and over. My favorite older cousin Terry, who I had resembled, allowed me to use his identification; to get into the club before I was twenty-one. My good friend did obtain his own identification from someone else that he had resembled; besides he was a little bit older than I was. This was really fun but it was small and had a lot of older gay men and women in the club, which was good but there was not enough action for us. So we did look forward to house parties that were going on around the city on club nights, which we did find. I then met my best friend Steven "Gaddie," which we did

THE TOTALITY OF DELIVERANCE

do everything together as well, including that same club but it was not giving us what we really needed at that time. So, we met a few friends who lived in Cincinnati who invited us to come and party at the clubs in their city, where we could enter in with our fake identifications too. It was just as small as ours but there were new faces and people that we did not know. At that time I was into the dating thing and actually I had a boy-friend in Indianapolis but he was locked up at the time. I did meet him at the club downtown but he was not from Indianapolis he was from Gary, Indiana. We were off and on for about five years, or should I say until I found out his dirty little secret that he was smoking crack behind my back without me knowing it. He was a guy that didn't care what gender, male or female that he was in a relationship with, because he was going to be the thug that he was regardless. While robbing, stealing, smoking, back and forth to jail and doing whatever it was that he wanted to do. You would have never thought that he was involved with another man because he did not portray that image and he certainly was not feminine at all. We were introduced by a woman that his brother was married to, that later became a close friend of mines that treated me as family. In which, her house began to be one of my weekly, partying and hangout spots.

    My best friend and I traveled almost every weekend

THE TOTALITY OF DELIVERANCE

to Cincinnati. Sometimes we would come home just to get more clothes and turn right back around and go back there. Besides, I had a few men that I was talking to and involved with in Cincinnati or should I say the "Nasty Natti!" I had lived my life with my player mentality going on, because I can remember going over my buddy house, in which I did have one guy in his bed room, another one on his couch in his living room, one more upstairs and the other one outside in the car waiting on me. Need I say more! On the contrary my best friend was no better than I was because I can recall a time when he caused us to get into a fight in that city, because he was talking to a guy and the guys lover behind his back. It was pure fun and freedom to do and to become whatever we wanted to be. In fact, both of these incidents had given us a warm welcome to their city and alerted them all, that we had arrived and were very live. Our friends in Cincinnati then turned us on to the gay club in Dayton, Ohio. Where you only had to be eighteen years of age to enter and also it closed at a later time than our clubs in Indianapolis. This club in Dayton was very different but more of our speed. The building had two clubs connected together. On the top floor was a gothic night club, where they would come wearing all black with leather, chains, wedding-gowns and strange attire. There would be fake bodies hanging from the ceiling of their dance floor and it was very dark, with

THE TOTALITY OF DELIVERANCE

predominantly all white people up there. Then there was down stairs, where there were predominantly young black men and women that was majority gay or lesbian. This club was very exciting being we didn't have anything like this in our city. Besides they loved us there and we loved being there. People would come from all over the surrounding cities just to party at this club. The club then took a turn for the worst because it began to have many of fights and all kinds of bad activities that caused it to close a few years later.

Now that I have begun same sex relationship situations, it began to lead from one thing to another. I was going deeper and deeper into one of the darkest lifestyles that anyone could ever live in, "Homosexuality." In the homosexual or lesbian lifestyle, there are many men and women who are without the parenting attention, that the normal people are raised up with, due to their choices or way of life. I myself became a victim of this partially, because I did not live the homosexuality lifestyle until I was a late teenager. My mother and my other family members treated me with love but yet I could still read their aura that was in the back of their minds, concerning my lifestyle. Many mothers and fathers have either walked out on their children, or gave up on them because of their lifestyle. With that being said, there are what is called or considered a "Gay Family" in this homosexual

THE TOTALITY OF DELIVERANCE

and lesbian lifestyle. The Family is incorporated with the same members that a regular family has mothers, fathers, sisters, brothers and so on. I myself became a mother of a very large family that had members in many of cities and states in the United States of America. I can remember going to high school with young men referring to me as mom or Amey when I had arrived, attended and left school.

The family began to grow larger and larger as I progressed into this lifestyle. I had to carry out normal motherly duties, as far as teaching them the ropes of this lifestyle and how to remain safe from all of the secret society defaults and defects that could cause them to either become, homeless, hopeless, sickly, or dead. This happens to be the major threat that most homosexuals have by participating in this lifestyle. Regardless, of whatever they are trying to do or become, indulging into this lifestyle without the proper leadership will result in one of these defects before it's all over. Being, I come from such a large blood born family, it was normal for me to understand this lifestyle because I had uncles, aunts, cousins and many other family members that had already indulged into it, before me. Not that they taught me or showed me how or what to do in this lifestyle, but I clearly understood that I could learn a lot from a "dummy!" Meaning some of the things that they would do or say that

THE TOTALITY OF DELIVERANCE

didn't work for them I knew wouldn't work for me. Sometimes when I was alone I would wonder why the people in my family was different from other families and why was it only certain members of our family that were extraterrestrial like myself? Speaking of extraterrestrial, my grandfather on my father side called me "E.T." as a child, because he said that I looked like E.T. the character off of that movie and he told me that my head was shaped funny just like his. He even bought me the E.T. bear that I carried around for years. Maybe he knew that I felt like E.T. inside and was extremely different from birth, on top of that movie being released in 1982; the same year that I was born. This put me on a deeper hunt to figure out why my life was so different. Only to find out later that this same sex nature was one of our family curses, that needed to be broken. So, I was quite familiar with how things should operate and most of the "do's and don'ts" of this total operation, of living this life. Not to mention all of the wisdom that God, my grandparents and my mom had given me, while learning from older family members, god mothers, as well as the many of friends of the family. I also adored and loved going over all of my aunts and uncles houses and staying a night. Mainly, because I loved each and every one of them, and it gave me a chance to learn how their living arrangements were set up as well as their way of life. I also enjoyed going over my mother's, friend's

THE TOTALITY OF DELIVERANCE

homes and learning from them too. I must mention that my mother had many great friends and Todd did too.

Then it finally happen, I made it to one of the best places of my life, high school graduation. I was going to make my family happy, I did it, I made it through all of those long years of tears, hard labor at school and working at the same time to make things all add up for my life. Well, that's what I had believed at least. I thought I had it all planned out, college then my own place, a nice job, next, I would find me a really good guy to be in a relationship with and live the life of my dreams. I did not necessarily know how long the relationship would last because I was still contemplating, on rather or not if I wanted some children of my own, later on in my life.

Part 2

(Late Teens/Early Twenties

Reprobate Mind ~ The Process

Of course things did not go as I had planned, because destruction did hit me once again. My grandfather was in a boat wreck accident, while he was fishing on a large body of water that caused his death. I should have known, because one month after my high school graduation, right before he had left to go fishing; I asked him to put air in one of my tires. He tried to tell me how to hook the air compressor machine up to his truck and do it myself. I told him that my hands are not made for such matter! I think it made him mad because he then began fussing at me and telling me the next steps that I should take in my life. He told me to make sure that I go to college and now that I was out of high school, I should get into my own apartment because of the relationship between me and my stepfather. He told me that I should not break up my mother's relationship with him, because when I had gotten older, I would not want to stay there

THE TOTALITY OF DELIVERANCE

with her and she would need some companionship. He then told me that he would help me get an apartment and help me through college, all the while he was grabbing his wallet to loan me some money for my car payment. He told me never to move too far away from home or Indiana because there would come a time in my life where I would need help from someone in the family. He also told me to always remember to keep God first, because he is able to see me through any situation that I might get into and needed help out of. He begun to speak as if he was never coming back, which was very strange but nevertheless he was only going fishing as he always does. It would have never entered into my heart that this would be the last time that I would hear his voice.

Very late that night the disturbing news had hit the family. That's when we found out that he had gotten into a terrible boat accident, along with one of his friends and one of my favorite cousins, Dewayne. It was later on that night, when we received the phone call that the boat turned over in the dark and that they could not find my grandfather. He was lost in a big body of water while doing one of his favorite sports besides hunting and going to church. Right, then and there, it's like I knew he was dead but somehow, I had the hope that he had been rescued by another boat that was out there on the water too. Or just maybe, he had swim out of the water with no

THE TOTALITY OF DELIVERANCE

way to call home to let us know that he was ok. All that night our family gathered together over my grandparent's house, praying and hoping that he was ok. We had a lot of confidence in him and the fact that he would have survived any and everything that came his way. We were all completely wrong. He had drowned underneath a large oil barge that carries oil from one place to another, by way of water. They could not find him that night, so the authorities had to wait until morning to put the oil barge in reverse, which caused his body to resurface to the top of the water. I later found out that his friend drowned as well, but my cousin Dewayne had swim out of the water. Instantly, I began to feel as if the only man that I had in my life had been taken away from me. What was I supposed to do now that my help was gone and my best friend too? Questions then began to repeat themselves over and over again in my head, until I begun to overwhelm my thinking process. "What was I going to do now?" "How am I going to make it with no male figure who, really cares about my life?" "What about my future, as a college graduate, that he wanted me to become?" Nevertheless, as I had dealt with my father being killed at an earlier age, I had gotten through it some way, somehow and now I must get through this one, too.

    The last words that my grandfather said, to me began to replay in my head, "get your own apartment but

THE TOTALITY OF DELIVERANCE

don't move too far away, because you are going to need your family!" He then told me to go to college and become very successful and that he would help me whenever I needed it, every step of the way. It was the middle of the summer when this accident took place, which means it was almost time to sign up for college in a few months. So, I would begin to try to accomplish the goals that he laid before me to reach, during that last conversation that we had discussed. First, I started by applying for college like my grandfather suggested and instructed me to do. In which I got accepted into Indiana University-Purdue University Indianapolis (IUPUI). This acceptance totally stunned me and made me extremely happy.

    Now, it was time for me to attend orientation at the college where the real labor of learning begins. My mother and I attended the orientation on a Saturday. Where there were so many people, we could hardly find a parking space. This was one of the most exciting events that could ever happen in my life and anyone else life, that had big dreams to follow, at 18 years of age. The last step that we had to do while in orientation was to go and talk to the financial office; but it was bad news from there. They told me that my father made way too much money for me to receive financial aid. "I'm confused, my father is deceased, there is no way this could be really possible!" Is what I had said. So she then read the name out loud and it was my

THE TOTALITY OF DELIVERANCE

mother's husband. I then told her," That is not my father that's my mother's husband!" She began to explain to me, that being my mother was married they would have to go off of the both of their incomes. My heart suddenly stopped and I really could not figure out what to say or what to do next. We had tried everything that we knew to do, but it was still a complete failure. The only thing that I could think about was all of the hard labor in school for twelve long hard years, for this terrible ending. For, I even had been placed in the "Who's Who Among American High School students book." There has got to be something that could be done! The last thing that she explained was a student will have to use their parent's taxes or income until the age twenty-four and that it was not the schools decision but it was the law.

    I was confused, broken, and disappointed that my hopes and dreams were now all over and down the drain forever. Well, they were over for at least six years because, I was only eighteen years of age and still had to wait until I was twenty-four years of age. I then went to the next step that I had planned to do on my list, which was to get my own apartment and continue on with my life. The search was not going so well, mainly, because I really did not have the credit that was needed at that time to get my own place and no cosigner as well. Not to mention, I really did not make the amount of money that

THE TOTALITY OF DELIVERANCE

the apartments required for tenants to have, so the only apartments that I could afford and would accept me were the low income apartments, (the projects). By this time, I had known that my grandfather and my father were rolling over in their graves probably fussing and cussing at me, both at the same time in the same manner. Reason being, I accepted the apartment in the projects and moved in with an attitude that I had become a victim to failure. I was in despair, all alone, on the other side of the city where I knew nothing about it. Not to mention, I was now living in the most dangerous apartments that our city had to offer at that time.

It was then, that the homosexual lifestyle did begin to transform me into another person that seemed to be good but was totally out of the will of God. Next, I began to travel to other cities heavily, to go to their gay clubs and to interact with other people of the same lifestyle, that I was living in. I can remember one night on our way to the club in Dayton, Ohio where there was my best friend, my gay father, a couple of the kids (gay boys) all riding in my car while I was driving. When one of the kids had drunk too much alcohol on our way there and he turned and threw up in the other kid's lap; that had on a bright white tee-shirt. At the same time that I was driving in a work zone and hit a pot hole and got a flat tire. I looked in the mirror and noticed red and blue lights

THE TOTALITY OF DELIVERANCE

flashing behind me. I'm thinking O Lord, have mercy on me, all of this at once and my license is suspended too. So I pulled over and waited for the cop to come to the window, but when he got there I told him that I had a flat tire, he then said "Ma'am will you step out of the car and open your trunk to get the spare tire and I will help you change it!" Of course everyone in the car started laughing, because I had a full mustache and beard but I did have a retro look with a twist. I had on a pair of "Dolce & Gabbana" pants that had blue jean material in the front with diamond cut gold sweater material in the back. My shirt was gold sweater diamond cut and my shoes were black clogs, with black straight shoulder length hair. I had gotten use to the cops calling me ma'am for some odd reason, although I had a very long beard and mustache. He then helped me put on the doughnut tire and allowed us to leave with no ticket, although my license was suspended with priors. Once we got into Dayton, Ohio it was raining hard, which made me slide into this wall on the ramp not far from the club. I just tapped on the dash board, laughed, backed up and kept going to the club; while everyone else just shook their heads and laughed at me. When it was time to leave the club I pulled out of the parking lot and immediately hit another pot hole and busted the doughnut tire that we had just put on. We were all shocked and so upset that it was funny to us. We

THE TOTALITY OF DELIVERANCE

were thinking what are we going to do in this little college city where everything is closed and no way home? So we called some of our friends from Cincinnati that was there. This was the wrong move because they had another car following them that had pulled out a gun on them as they pulled up behind my car. Now we are sitting here on a flat with a car riding pass us with a gun hanging out of their window pointing it at us. Yes, I had my gun but we were stuck downtown in that little city with nowhere to run and no get way car to roll out with. Thanks to God they kept driving and realized we had nothing to do with their situation and that we were only still there because I had a flat tire. Next, one of my friends from Dayton came and took my best friend to steal somebody else's tire off of their car that looked like it could fit my car. They brought the tire back with them but it did not fit. So they went and took another tire from someone else's car who was probably in a deep sleep, this tire was the right size. We got home four hours later than normal. Next me and my best friend would start to travel to Chicago often. We had already traveled to Cincinnati and Dayton. Now it was time for the other side of our highway, where everything was live, fresh and a new start. Chicago was much faster than Indianapolis, Cincinnati and Dayton put together. We got along well with everyone, besides we were from another city, we looked fresh and were a new species to

THE TOTALITY OF DELIVERANCE

them. I loved Chicago, I even moved there for a while but it was too much in some areas and in others areas it was just unrealistic and too uncomfortable to live.

I then started using drugs, like marijuana, cigarettes, alcohol, and ecstasy pills, in which they were one of the key players in this lifestyle. Well for me and my friends at least. Next, I began to indulge myself into the night life even heavier, along with partying and traveling at the drop of a dime. However, I did try to maintain a job from time to time. I mean after all, it still took money to survive this extraordinary lifestyle that I had taken on. As, I begin to progress into this lifestyle, I noticed that there was a certain way of life that most people would live by. Just to survive in a society that did not really accept the way that we lived. In which, really made it very hard to get hired at a job or to either keep the job because of the judgmental society that we lived in. So they found a fast and easier way to make money to survive in this lifestyle. "Fraud," it was the one thing that runs heavily and rapidly in this lifestyle throughout all of its generations. It was so heavy, that majority of my friends or associates of this lifestyle had either been questioned by the FEDs or spent some time in prison for this crime. It was God, who kept me through these trying times in my life because I had never, really done any of the fraudulent activities before. Mainly because I always worked at a legitimate job before

THE TOTALITY OF DELIVERANCE

totally indulging into this lifestyle and I did complete and obtain a high school diploma to back me up. In which, it was very rare to run into a homosexual with a high school diploma in those days, because of the slander during school. After all, I made a lot of work history from working at so many jobs and by starting to work at such an early age. First, I began by working at a catering job for the INDY 500 race Inn and a very famous pizza shop at the age of fourteen, not one but two jobs. Then at the age of sixteen I was a bank teller downtown working through a program that had started from school and a cashier at a big toy store. Next I was a teacher at a daycare and a cashier at sears outlet store at seventeen years of age. By the time I was eighteen years of age, I was working as a collections representative for a financing center. Then I would just move from job to job because I was not stable, but I did obtain many of skills underneath my belt, after all of these jobs. I received plenty of experience in these skills; catering, warehouse, retail, cashier, restaurants, teaching kids, classroom assistants, computers and even plenty of salesmen positions and many more.

    However, our family had a talent that we used as a skill that ran through the family, in which it was hairstyling. My mother was a licensed, barber and stylist with plenty of skill and artistry work with her hands, even on paper too. In fact, our home where we did live while

THE TOTALITY OF DELIVERANCE

growing up, was one house down from my grand-parent's house, that had a beauty and barber salon connected to it. Yes, I was blessed with the same talent that the rest of the family have. I'd gained my first client at the age of fourteen and would continue to grow every time someone else, who seen that client's hair would ask them, "who did it and what is their number?" This would always be my side hustle throughout my lifetime. That is what I had said, and that is what I had done, most of the time in the projects where I lived. I had plenty of clients because of the easy access to my home as well as my availability to do their hair at any time. If they had the money, I had the time and skill and I was only one phone call away. The projects were my home, for about two and a half years. Then I stayed with a few friends for a little while until I moved into my grandmother's house, that she lived in when I was younger. It was the house with the space, where the beauty and barber salon was located.

    Just a few months before I moved out on my own, there was a huge soy bean factory that was located on the next street over from our homes; that exploded. This soy bean factory literally blew up and caused a lot of damage to the neighborhood and its surroundings. I was not at home with the rest of the family when this incident had taken place; I had only seen the end results from the explosion the next day. I was over my favorite aunt Nora's

THE TOTALITY OF DELIVERANCE

who was my stepfather's sister. She would always allow me to come and stay over there with her son Rhyon and her husband Wayne. They always made me feel very special and loved. I really loved them and I loved the get away with them, because it was a relief and a break from my side of the family and my side of the city. The majority of my aunts and uncles lived on the same street or the next street over from my grandparent's house, because they all had such a close relationship to my grandparents. With our family being so large, majority of the homes on the street that we lived on, as well as the next two streets over, but not excluding that neighborhood entirely; had belonged to many of my relatives. This was not a very wealthy area but it was sufficient enough for my family to live and survive all together. After the explosion took place, it provided away out of this area for the entire family, by a law suit that the neighborhood had won in court. The explosion ruined most of the homes in that area and even if it did not, they still offered them the option to move into a new home in another location; because of the radical explosion. My family took the offer and they all moved during the time that I lived in the projects, into bigger and better homes. This was really good because most of the homes in that area were older and roach infested. I can remember going over one of my aunt's house where I was scared to sit down a bag of food,

THE TOTALITY OF DELIVERANCE

even though it was wrapped up. Mainly, because I knew that some roaches were going to get inside of that bag somehow. I got busy and put the bag down anyways, and as I already had known, I opened up my bag and there were two big ugly roaches crawling in my food. I got mad and threw the whole bag away!

My grandmother owned her home at that time so she allowed me to move in there, once I could not take the pain of the projects anymore. I was not only living the homosexual lifestyle, but I had begun to become a product of my horrible environment. Low income apartments, doing hair at home in the kitchen, food stamps, fighting, drugs, and a fraudulent lifestyle, was getting to me and pulling me down. Not to mention, I was not going to church as often as I did before. I then moved into her house that approximately had twelve rooms there, including the two big areas that were added on, for the beauty and barber salon. This entitled me to much more space for many of my friends to come and live with me, as a regular family would. Not to mention, I had already taken on the name Mother Amey or simply Ms. Amey because of the motherly and womanly duties and role that I had taken on throughout this lifestyle experience; by this time. Being, I understood that there were so many young men and women that were living on

THE TOTALITY OF DELIVERANCE

the streets, from getting put out of their homes by their parents, because of indulging into this lifestyle.

There is one thing that I must admit, and that is my mother definitely showed her love for me in-spite of the lifestyle that I chose to live. In which, it made me feel the need to show others who struggled with the lack of parenting attention, the love that they could not get from their mom, as a growing young man or woman. After all, I had gotten my hands on a house with many rooms, and by that time I had developed what we considered "kids," referring to sons, daughters, sisters, brothers, uncles and aunts. Not only here in Indiana, but also living in many other states in America. So, of course I allowed many of them to live with me, some from other states and many from Indiana.

There was a new recreation that I had discovered when I moved to Chicago for a little while, which was called the "Ballroom scene." A function in which many of the different gay families would come together to battle other gay families in different category's, where you win trophies, cash prizes and a name for yourself and your gay family. This event is held in most cities in America and it is an underground event that takes place normally late nights when the rest of the world is sleep or doing something not pertaining to this function. The different

THE TOTALITY OF DELIVERANCE

categories are equaled to, but not only modeling, beauty competitions, vogue or dance competitions and many other different categories that are held at these functions. The Ballroom scene or "Ball" was created because of the neglect to the real world and the lack of opportunity to be whatever they wanted to be; because of their choice of lifestyle. In return, they would come together to create their own environment or achievements just to have something to be proud of. This did become such a major part of my life and the friends that I hung with, lives too. If you are not careful the "Ball Scene" will take over your life, because of the attention, admiration, creativity and much more exciting opportunities that takes place at these events. With that being said, we had formed a "house" here in Indiana, myself and one of my favorite cousins Opey. In which, a house is what the family is actually called or referring to. When I came back from Chicago, I told Opey about the ball scene that was there and how they were voguing. He instantly knew what I was talking about and asked could we start one here for his birthday and I told him yes. So we did and it took a lot of practicing, training and teaching; in order for any house to be successful at the ball. Now, with me moving into my grandmother's house the space and opportunity there, allowed us to obtain a chance to become really great at what we did together. Not, only at the ball but also our development as young gay African American men and women as well.

    Living together, helped us to have the family love that we thought we needed or was missing from our lives. As I lived the motherly role, I had to have a very strategic mindset. As well as, a way of carrying myself; in order to fit the character that I was portraying to be. Personality wise, I had to be loving, caring, understanding, always compromising the duties of my real life to fit this lifestyle; in which it had taken over me as well. I lost a lot of things living in this lifestyle and endured many of hardships on different occasions, as a result from indulging into it so deeply. To name some, I can remember almost getting locked up for harboring minors, when in actuality they really ran away or got kicked out of their parents or guardians homes, because of their choice to live in this lifestyle. I can remember fighting for others, going to court to help get them out of their troubles and I even remember a murder case where one of my friends had used my gun in an altercation that they were in. I had come to the understanding that trouble and havoc was a part of the majority of everyone's lives, that I dealt with in this lifestyle.

    On the contrary, I can remember a lot of things that were great that happened, starting in that house; once all

THE TOTALITY OF DELIVERANCE

of us moved together. Like my twenty-first birthday bash. It was held there at my grandmother's old house where there were almost one to two hundred of my friends and kids there. The television station "HBO," came and took some footage from my party and played it on national television. In which, we did have a really nice time except about midnight when I had to break into my own bedroom door, where one of the young men that I knew was using his mouth on one of my male strippers. When I open the door he literally spit semen on my floor. I picked him up by his throat, choking him until he was blue and purple in the face; until the crowed stopped me, and I made him clean it up. Then I threw him out of the party. I can remember holding an after party there after our first house ball that lasted for two days, with the third day being the after set of the after party. I even remember the meetings and practices we held there at that house periodically that was so fun. Probably because we were so high on marijuana and drunk off of alcohol. There would be so much smoke; I believe we had our own clouds inside of the house. I stayed there for about two and a half years. Next, I would have to go and stay with my grandmother at her new house. She had just found out that her sugar diabetes was getting the best of her and many other health problems, as time progressed in her life. I did not go alone by myself because I had brought my lifestyle and my kids with me.

THE TOTALITY OF DELIVERANCE

Yes, we still held family meetings, vogue practices and everything else that came along with the lifestyle. My birth family treated them as real family members of ours and some of them also helped me to encourage them. I believe it was because of the love that our family had shown to everyone, no matter what lifestyle they live. As well as the respect that the kids had shown me with the title or name that I indeed earned. While I was living there, I traveled heavily from city to city and state to state making a name for myself that carried across the country. Places like Detroit, Michigan. This place felt like home, it was ghetto and no matter where we had hung out at, it was all in the hood. The people there were so nice and so hospitable with so much love to give; to me at least. I got along with most of them, as they did treat me as family. I fell in love with Detroit and stayed there for a while, it was like my second home. I did encounter many of tragic incidents, dealing with my cars as I traveled there sometimes, because of the constant visits. Incidents like; being stuck on the side of the road where I had to spend a night in the car, stranded in other cities, pushing my vehicle to my destination, blown gaskets, riding with no axle on one side of the car and I can even remember having to change my own alternator five times just to make it home. It didn't matter as long as I could get to Detroit I did not care. That's where I had met my gay mother, "The Goddess!" He was not a drag queen but just a butch queen as I was. (Butch Queen- A gay male that is neither extremely feminine, nor extremely masculine and can easily portray both mannerisms. He was the mother of that city, as I was the mother of Indianapolis. But it didn't stop there, because I started visiting many of cities while attending balls everywhere like, Washington D.C., Kentucky, Ohio, Los Angeles, NYC, Pittsburgh, New Jersey, Atlanta, St. Louis, and of course all of Indiana, Chicago and many other cities. I can even remember a trip to Hawaii with my Detroit family.

    I lived with my grandmother for about two years and then I was approved for affordable housing. This was a major blessing for me at this time of my life, because I really was not working and maintaining a stable job. Yet, I was still making money, just the ruthless way and by doing hair. I then moved into a one bedroom apartment where I was still progressing with the lifestyle but I was growing in age. I began wanting to do more for myself in the real world and work towards my early childhood dreams, instead of what I was doing. I was selling drugs, trying to make a quick dollar to keep up with the lifestyle that I was living. It was ok for the first few years but one night I had a gathering at the apartment and with just a regular knock at the door, I answered it and to my surprise; I had a silver, shiny, piece of metal that rested on the center of my

THE TOTALITY OF DELIVERANCE

forehead, it was a gun. I was being robbed at gun point by two guys that had caught me off guard. They did not get much, but to have the tip of a gun resting on my forehead was more than enough reasons for me to stop selling drugs. I begin to open my eyes and thank God after this situation because I really could have been dead. Although I prayed and thanked God much, this was not the first time that I had come into contact with a gun situation, at close range. One night, a few years prior to this robbery when I was staying in Chicago, I was driving my car with three of my friends from there. When we pulled over to a corner by the projects that were near downtown, a guy walked up to the passenger window of my car and asked us, "are yall some kind of fags or something?" That's when one of the guys in the back seat yelled out the window, "yeah we some fags and what you gone do?" The guy reached behind his back and pulled out a shiny nine millimeter gun and started shooting close range. I pulled out my gun that was hidden in the steering wheel, where the spot for the horn was. We pulled off and as I was driving a hundred miles per hour down the street, one of my friends noticed that he was shot. He was my gay father Lavell. After we had gotten him to the hospital and realized where he had been shot at, I then realized that the bullet really should have gone through my head. With the way that he turned to dodge the bullets and the way

THE TOTALITY OF DELIVERANCE

that I ducked my head to dodge the bullets, put my head next to his ankle where the bullet went all the way through and launched to the floor, right before my head. I prayed and thanked God after this shooting as well. I then came back home a few days later.

Next, I signed up for school to become a medical assistant. It went swell, but a little challenging because the way that my life was set up, it was hard to maintain both. I still managed to graduate and then begun to work in the many of different fields that the degree carried. Yet, I was still living in this lifestyle of darkness and still living kind of loose too. Loose from dealing with all of the different kids that I felt fully responsible for that had gotten me into all kinds of illegal situations and ungodly things. Although, I had a job in the medical field, I still carried my hair clients with me everywhere I moved to, no matter what side of town I was on. When I sat down and added up the total amount of money that I had made from my hairstyling clientele monthly; I somehow was making more money than my full time job in this field of work. In which, that was mind boggling because I made a pretty good amount of money in the medical field at that present time.

Then out of nowhere my mind would flash back to when I was younger and would always watch my entire family style hair in the salon that was connected to the house. I can remember wanting to be like my favorite aunt Sheila and my mom doing hair, making that fast money the legal way. Again, I would have to go back to school and get my cosmetology license, while I had just graduated from medical school in 2007. Another, major stumbling block did come to my mind, as I thought about the school that I would attend. How would I get the funds to pay for school and did I have what it takes to get it? I then begin to call around to the different schools, to find out what their requirements were. I found out that the requirements were not all that bad besides the class room schedule being all day from eight thirty in the morning until five o'clock pm. As well as losing a lot of my free time from having to attend school almost six days a week, for the next year and a half. "Geesh," that would really put me out of reach from the ball scene, the kids for a very long time and my clients that mostly would come during school hours. I decided not to pursue it while I was in the current situations of my life. Besides, I was about to make a legendary status in the ball room scene as I continued to attend the balls. In which, one of the main goals in the ball room scene is to become a legend and to obtain the wonderful admiration from the whole scene, from state to state. I felt, I had obtained that from the beginning because I had the finest kids, I came in dressed well; normally some kind of label on and always some kind of

THE TOTALITY OF DELIVERANCE

stunning shoe. With a whole new attitude and didn't mind shutting down the ball rather if it was from winning a trophy, me pulling out my gun, getting chopped and not leaving the runway, or and fighting.

Next, I would use creative thinking to learn how to add more people to the large clientele that I already had gained over the years. Being, I started building up my clientele during my early teenage years. I managed to still maintain every one of my clients, although I had gone through many of changes in my living arrangements. I then begin to have tattoo parties, house parties and attended many of hair shows with my aunt Sheila, in Atlanta for a well, known product company.

My life had begun to get quite interesting with the way things were going. It was the money, all of the strange people that were entering into my life now, and a live in, same sex relationship. My relationships usually lasted a long time if they acted right, was extremely faithful, knew how to treat me and made some money of their own. The majority of them last for at least two years, because of my faithfulness and over powering love, that I regenerated from my family's bloodline. The relationship that I was in at this time did begin to take the turn for the worst. We began to have trust issues and entirely too much arguing and fighting. Just like the rest of the relationships with

THE TOTALITY OF DELIVERANCE

other men, this one had come to an end as well. In which, I got tired of this same rotation of falling in and out of love with a man. It seemed like same sex relationships just did not work because they would all come to an end no matter how great they started out.

    I then begin a new chapter in my life where I had gotten into a relationship with a stud, woman. In which, is a woman who is masculine or the dominant person in the same sex female relationships. This relationship had brought my memory back to my early high school years, where I was in a relationship with a female that I did not choose to pursue. Not to mention I had already experience sex with a female and male by the age of eighteen. This relationship last for about a year and a half. I was content with her but she had other things that she wanted to do with her life. It was time for me to be happy again, alone while enjoying my space and opportunity that was calling my name. Now, I really started going to the clubs and traveling very heavy, for my life did turn into sex, drugs and rock n' roll. At least that's the best way that I could explain it. Needless to say, it was done in a sophisticated manner. For, I was mother and not just mother but I was rewarded mother of the year for as long as I was in the scene. With that, I had to still carry myself in a respectable manner that called for immediate respect from others. When I attended the clubs and parties and

THE TOTALITY OF DELIVERANCE

balls I was normally ushered in with many of my kids, prepared and ready to do whatever the moment had called for at that time. This is what I loved about each and every one of them, I had their back and they had mine. Our love for each other was so genuine you could see it even if you did not know us personally. Which means, wherever I lived that's where most of them hung at, no matter what time or day, even in the small one bedroom apartment too.

    I then found another friend that caused my feelings to get so deep into him that I lost myself. I don't know what it was that caused me to feel this way about him but it had led, to one of the most life changing experiences, I feel that anyone could ever go through. It was a proven fact that I was looking for someone to clearly love me in a manner that is undeniable. This was one of my biggest down falls and hardest issues at that point and time of my life. It felt like, I just could not find that right person with the type of love that I was looking for. I tried so many men and women that I felt like it was no one out there for me, man or woman; in this state or any state on earth. I had tried relationships in plenty of cities and states but honestly, I did not trust anyone by the time that I entered into this last, same sex relationship. It was definitely not easy getting me to open up after the guy before him and that stud woman that was unfaithful. I did not want to

THE TOTALITY OF DELIVERANCE

allow anyone else to even get close to the inside of my heart. This guy was different, he had played hard to get but I wasn't thirsty for anyone anyways, it was not my character. He clearly came back to me after he turned down my approach the weekend before, at the club. He re-approached me, the next weekend at that same club with a mouth full of apologies and asking me out on a date. Our relationship started smooth, mainly because he was from another small city in Indiana and he really did not know that many people; because he was new to the homosexual lifestyle. I was cool with that because I really didn't trust anybody, anyways. Not to mention the last male relationship that I was in, my partner ended up cheating on me with one of my kids, after a two year relationship. In which the office manager at my apartments actually, was the one who really caught him cheating on me. They were in the exercising room connected to the office. Automatically, I felt humiliated after my office manager called me to the office, only to deliver me a message like this. I fought my boyfriend and chased him with my gun and he ran and hid over my family house until they sent him back home to Chicago.

Following that incident; caused a huge massive war inside of me, debating on loving anyone anymore or allowing someone to even love me. I didn't want anything,

THE TOTALITY OF DELIVERANCE

from what was considered a relationship to a live in man, or any kids that are really vipers from this point on.

This next guy was different, it's like he was sent specifically to me, for me but I did not know that this was about to change my life forever. This guy was a part of God's strategy to get me into his Kingdom way of thinking. I really do believe this because, only God could have blocked what I was about to do, if I would have honored what that evil, wicked, familiar voice that was controlling me at that time, instructed me to do. The guy that I was dating was cheating on me with someone else. After, all of the measures that he would go through or use to make sure that I was not cheating on him, I just could not believe, that he had done this to me. One snowy night, one of my sons called me from the club and told me that he had just seen the guy that I was dating, come in with another guy. That it appeared to be definitely more than just a normal friendship because of how close they were dancing and etc. I knew it to be true, because two other witnesses confirmed this was happening, including the guy that he was messing around with. In which, I tried to ignore it because in the homosexual lifestyle, it is very normal for people to pass judgment on relationships and lies, to cause confusion in happy homes. Although, I really wanted to trust him, because I was always taught, that there is no such thing as a relationship without trust.

THE TOTALITY OF DELIVERANCE

When I got the phone call, I immediately called him and begin to discuss this situation, that's when the guy somehow got on the phone and started arguing with me. As if it did not matter about our relationship that we were in. We argued until the early a.m., that next morning. That's when I heard that evil voice tell me to go over there and kill them both. To sum it up he lived down the street from me, which made it even easier because, I was ready to fight and kill. Keep in mind I am Germany's brother. So I went to his apartment and the other guy would not come off of the porch to fight me. He had screamed out loud, that he was not going to fight me; I then went back to get my gun. That evil voice began to speak to me, he told me to wait before I kill both of them. That there were two other people that made me mad with some disrespectful things they had done earlier that week. That evil voice told me to kill those two first, then the guy I was in a relationship with and last the guy that he was cheating with. Being, the state of mind that I was in at that time, made it sound like the perfect thing to do. So, I agreed to do it until that voice told me that I must promise to kill myself when I was done killing them. I thought it over, let it settle in my system for a minute, then I yelled out no deal and begin to scream out the name of Jesus and continued to call on God the father to help me with this situation.

THE TOTALITY OF DELIVERANCE

I began to say to myself, "this is it and I am through with relationships no matter what the gender may be!" I had started praying, praising, worshiping, and going to church on an everyday basis from this day forward. I would find some church to attend, no matter where it was located or what kind of denomination it was. Daily, I would only watch the Christian networks on television and only listen to gospel music on the radio. My insides had a need for this kind of feeling and feeding of the spirit. I even went back to my family church that I had belonged to earlier in my life. I got re-baptized again and began to try to find out who, and what I was created to do and live for. I needed real help because I was deeply hurt beyond measure and could not find the comfort that my heart was longing for. As I went to church it seemed as If, the preacher would always preach a good message on how God will make away for you. That somehow he will bring you out of whatever you were in that you did not like. This was not helping, I thought that maybe I needed to read the bible myself, and complete new membership classes to help me further my approach to God. I was so hungry and thirsty for him that I was doing any and everything just to get his attention. Besides, I was taught that praising God and worshiping him is what he desires and that he would answer you because it was a form of knocking on his door. I then began the new membership classes at the

THE TOTALITY OF DELIVERANCE

family Baptist church that I was attending once again. One night I read a few scriptures that explained that everyone who wanted to go to heaven must be water baptized and baptized with the Holy Spirit (Fire).(John 3:5) After all, I remembered that I did learn at an early age, that the red letters in the Holy Bible were words that Jesus spoke himself. Also, I was told that if I did not believe anything else in the bible, that I could believe and trust those red words.

The next day while I was in new member's class at the family Baptist church, the teacher who was one of the ministers at the church asked a question. This question really had me confused, although he asked the whole class. Not confused about the answer of the question, but why would a preacher ask this question, when I thought this is what he should be preaching about. "He asked us to raise our hands if we believe that we have to be baptized before we die to go to heaven?" I raised my hand, but I noticed that I was the only one who had raised my hand in the class room. Then he said, "Why do you believe that we have to be baptized in order to go to heaven?" I then explained to him that the night before, I had just read in the Holy Bible that not only did Jesus say that we had to be baptized with water and the Holy Spirit but I had read it other places in the Holy Bible as well. He told me that I was wrong and he began to explain to me the incident in

THE TOTALITY OF DELIVERANCE

the Holy Bible, where one of the men on the cross next to Jesus, asked Jesus to remember him when he got to his kingdom. Jesus told him that he would be in paradise with him. Ok, now I'm really confused a preacher is telling me that the instructions in Gods Holy word is not accurate and that I did not understand what I was reading. So as class went on I was boggled in my mind. I notice that right before the class ended, the teacher gave us a story from when he was teaching one of his first Sunday school classes. He told us that the Holy Spirit convicted him because he was not baptized yet. That he had to stop teaching class and needed to go and get baptized before he could carry on with his teachings. Everyone in the class room then turned and looked at me, while the class room dismissal bell rung. Immediately, I said to myself, "that's exactly what I thought, how are you going to be a teacher of Gospel, but teach against God's, Holy Word!" I then knew that this was not the church for me any longer, but what church would I attend now?

Part 3

(Late Twenties)

Praise and Worship ~ Spiritually Walking

Power From ON High ~ Perseverance

    I would now begin to go on a search for a new church home but I was raised up under the Baptist church belief system, so that was more of what I was looking for or leaning towards. Then this small voice came to my mind that said, "I will show you which one to go to!" Next I begin visiting other church's with different family members and friends. Some of the churches came very close to what I was looking for but yet, they still were not it. After a few weeks of going from church to church, I ran into one of my old running buddies in the mall from the past. He was praising God with a loud shout, he was so radical that I stopped and asked him, "What's wrong with you?" He began to explain to me that he was still excited about the night before, from a sermon that his preacher had preached. I was amazed because I knew the guy but praising God was not a part of what I had known about him. Not to mention I was friends with him for years but

THE TOTALITY OF DELIVERANCE

this part of him was surprising and shocking to me. So, I asked him, "What church do you go to?" He told me, "Mt. Zion Apostolic Church," which brought up a question in my mind. I was Baptist and the things that I had heard about apostolic churches did not sound too appealing to me. As, I was leaving the mall and approaching my home, I called my mother while she was still at work and there was a woman praising God so loud in her background that It over threw my mother's voice. I asked her, "who is that woman making all that noise and where are you at?" She told me that she was still at work and that the woman praising in the background was still on fire from her preacher's message last night at her church. I told her to ask the lady "what church do she attend?" Nevertheless, it was Mt. Zion Apostolic Church! I then told my mom what had just happened, at the mall with my friend and asked her a rhetorical question, "could this be a sign from God?"

Early the next morning, while I was styling one of my clients hair, he called one of his female friends. She was praising God so loud in the phone that he really could not get any words through to her at all. In which he was getting very upset with her, so he asked her what was wrong with her? She told him that her spirit was still on fire from Sunday night service at her church. He then told her, that he was trying to schedule a time where he could get some sex from her and that she needed to stop

THE TOTALITY OF DELIVERANCE

praising God. But she kept praising God anyways. That's when he had gotten very irritated and frustrated and then decided to hang up on her. I begged him to call her back, so he could ask her; "what church does she attend?" He did and of course she said, "Mt. Zion Apostolic Church!" That was the third strike! I felt like this was the church that God was directing me to attend, so I did. Mt. Zion was everything that my heart and spirit was longing for, the moment that I stepped into its atmosphere. I had already known in my spirit, that once I arrived at this church, it would help me arise to the place in God that I was yearning for. Not to mention, the bishop there was my type of preacher. He was Bishop Lambert Gates Sr., and his name had expressed to me how the church made me feel. It was the feeling of this church becoming the "Gate" way to the next level of my life in God, through Christ Jesus; which is where I was trying to go.

    I then began, to attend two of the three services, which were the afternoon and evening services. Yet, there was still something that I was confused on and that was my lifestyle. I did not really notice anyone there that I could probably talk to about my lifestyle. Being, I did not know anyone there, besides the woman that my mother had worked with and my friend from the past that told me about the church. Surly, they could not help me personally, but I was tired of the way that I was living and the Bishop at that church would preach directly to me

THE TOTALITY OF DELIVERANCE

about my lifestyle without him knowing it. One evening service, about three months into attending the church, the Bishop made a statement that caught my attention. He said, "If you are gay? Being a homosexual or lesbian and you are looking for a church home, you can come here I will be your pastor!" I turned and looked at my friend Tony with a surprised smile! That was all I needed and exactly what I was looking for in a church. I then went up to the altar and told them that I wanted to be a part of this church family. The altar worker was a woman that asked me, "Have you ever been baptized in the name of the Lord Jesus Christ? Also, do you have the Holy Spirit with the evidence of speaking in other tongues?" I told her that I had just been baptized a few months ago but I did not speak in other tongues and that I wanted to speak in other tongues. It was then that I was baptized for the third time in my life. I was baptized as a child around the age of twelve and then I was re-baptized at the family church, a few months before Mt. Zion's baptismal. When I went down in the water at Mt. Zion, I felt something that I had never felt before. It took over my body and to my surprise it was the Holy Spirit like never before. Next, the altar woman tarried with me for a little while and that's when I began to speak in other tongues. That night I did not go to the church alone, I had one of my besties Tony and one of my sons Rodney with me whom, once I gotten baptized they did so as well. My aunt Sheila was there too. My Son Chad joined a few months later. We would all talk on the phone while watching the same gospel station on

THE TOTALITY OF DELIVERANCE

television, all day and all night praising God and listening to every sermon that came on; after this service.

I then moved into another building that was still in the same apartment complex, where I could feel a new me. Being, I still felt a tug of the homosexuality lifestyle tugging at me trying to stop me from progressing in God. Not to mention, I had heard so many different things about religion that I really didn't know what I was doing or where my life was headed. One night when I was riding alone, on my way home from leaving a church service, I began to talk to myself or thought that I was talking to myself. That's when I recognized that God had joined in on the conversation too. I thought about how I would live now that I have been filled with the Holy Spirit, because no one that I knew of had really done anything like this before. I knew this because they were all telling me that, "it does not take all of that, and that God made you like you are, just accept it and be happy." Instantly God begin to speak to me when I was talking to myself in the car. He started discussing with me how the lifestyle that I was living was not in his will for my life and that it would never work between me and another guy for real. He told me that the life style that I was living would not and could not ever inherit his heavenly kingdom. I began to discuss with him how I was a loving and giving person and how I receive so many young men and women and bless them with whatever I have or can do for them. He said, "That is why you reap such a great harvest because you sow so many good seeds, but that still will not inherit the

THE TOTALITY OF DELIVERANCE

Kingdom!" He began to tell me that the bible was 100% true and correct and that he has repentance for this type of lifestyle but those who live it will not be in heaven with him. I then said, "I was born like this!" He said, "You're right and that is why I stated that you must be born again or you will not inherit the kingdom of God!" I was driving down the street alone, approaching a road where I could not go straight anymore. I either had to turn left or right. In which, this also was a sign to my life that it was time to turn and go in the right direction. As I approached this dead end, God spoke to me and said, "The choice is yours and everyone has the right to choose which way they are going to go in life; in which that determines your final destination when you leave earth!" I begin to ask and discuss with God, how was I going to explain this to the people? People like my kids, my friends and family that believed we were born like this and that God loves everyone, even those who believes that Jesus died so that we could live this homosexual lifestyle. God begin to explain to me that the lifestyle that we were living in, was an evil spirit and he told me to tell them that "the only spirit that will reside in the kingdom of God or Heaven is the Holy Spirit." I went home with a lot on my mind. I had heard so many different things about this lifestyle, that it put me in total confusion. The voice that I'd just heard had me in total shock but yet comfort because I knew it was God. I then begin my research. I started out by going to my book shelf that was in my bedroom. I attempted to get my bible that I had when I did go to church on a weekly basis, when I was younger. That's when a bible coloring book fell

THE TOTALITY OF DELIVERANCE

out to the floor and open up to two pages, one of them being the Samson and Delilah story out of the bible. In which Samson had power in his hair that he was not suppose, to tell anyone where his power came from. But, Delilah had tricked him into telling her where his power came from and caused him to kill himself. The other page had the bible story about Jacob and his dream with the angels going to and fro, heaven to earth by way of a ladder. The two stories prompt me to go and read about them in the Holy Bible, but I could not really conclude anything yet.

    That's when I decided to start from the beginning of the bible reading every chapter word for word verse to verse. In which, I did read the entire book. This struck something in my mind that made me go back to the first thing that I had really learned about spirits. Being, God had just started speaking to me about spirits in the earlier car conversation. I remember, learning about the Indians who supposedly smoked out of a peace pipe to get in touch with the spirit realm and that they had direct contact with the spirits when they did smoke. "What did they put in the peace pipes?" Was my next question, in which I began to research what they had smoked and my ending results, was marijuana. I then read that God instructed his people in the bible to go into a secret place or closet to pray and meditate on his word both night and day. As well as build him an, altar. I then began to put all of these things together to find out what would happen. I

THE TOTALITY OF DELIVERANCE

first tried smoking marijuana out of a pipe but when I would do that I would feel a peace come over me; but there were too many voices that I heard and so many different things going through my mind at that time. It had all became too confusing for me. Not to mention, I could not remember the things that would come to my mind when the high that I had went away. This did not work as I thought it would or maybe it was peaceful but not quit what I was searching for. Which, I was searching for God to show up himself, in the smoke or air and speak to me. Next, I began to make an altar in my closet, praying to God every day and specifically at midnight. I would go every night praying, begging and pleading with him to reveal himself to me. Being, that I had heard so many controversial things about Jesus, by this time; I felt that I needed to hear from God himself, nothing more and nothing less.

    The search went on perhaps one month before God finally showed up and spoke to me with an audible voice. He told me that I had found him through prayer but I must come through his son Jesus the Christ. Then I accepted the fact that Jesus was lord and the myths were true. That's when Christ Jesus showed up in my closet. I had one candle lit that had a cross on it and with my eyes closed I saw a very bright light with a man with a very familiar face. The face that you see at most of the stores that was

THE TOTALITY OF DELIVERANCE

supposed to be Jesus. Finally, it was him whose voice that I heard say hello and welcome my son. He began to speak to me about how his father told him that I was looking for God and that I was ready for a new life. He began to tell me things that I had come through to get to the point where I was and how much he love me. There was a feeling of peace and so much joy I could hardly even move. So much, that I had never felt like this before and I did not want this feeling to ever leave me. When I came out of the closet, I had a smile on my face that made my jaws hurt from smiling so long and so hard. I had just come into contact with the almighty God, of the entire universe. Wow! Who am I that he would come and reveal himself to me? I went to sleep that night and had a dream for the first time in years. The dreams started to direct me from day to day and to prepare me for things that would happen later on in my life. I would later begin to go in my prayer closet and just talk to him because I knew that he heard me but I did not learn how to listen to his voice yet. Yet, he still managed to answer all of my prayers one by one and from day to day.

    I then decided to sign up for cosmetology school. It was very challenging because I had just begun a new life with Jesus Christ and now a new career, the professional way. I was very familiar with the work, but adapting to being, around so many different people and personalities,

THE TOTALITY OF DELIVERANCE

on a day to day basis; all day long was getting the best of me. The majority of people there were women and because I was still on fire with Jesus Christ, daily I would come into school with an outrageous praise; shouting, singing, dancing, preaching or praying. The praise in me would not stop no matter what the teachers or the other students would say. I was prone to giving God the praise and glory all day and night and it was not about to stop now. Besides, it would be best for me to continue praising him than letting the old me resurface; due to the unreligious peers and teachers that I would have to deal with for the next year and a half. In-spite of all the ungodliness that I had to deal with there at school, it was not enough to knock me off of my journey with Jesus Christ. Besides, I had made some promises to God and he had made some to me and under any circumstance or situation I was going to keep my promises to him. As I began to approach the middle of the year in cosmetology school; I began to grow in wisdom as well as my relationship with God. After all, that's all that I would do every day, is talk to God and look and listen for the signs and dreams of him speaking back to me. Until one day, I was in my prayer closet praying and had gotten deep into the spirit realm. I felt a touch on my back shoulder, which was scary because I was in the closet alone with the door shut and no lights on but my candle was lit, and no one

THE TOTALITY OF DELIVERANCE

else there at the house. I jumped up immediately looking for whom and what had just touched me. I always wanted Jesus to touch me but this was a non-expectant touch in the dark from behind. Later on when I had gone to sleep, I noticed that the dreams begun to be more vivid, more realistic and more dreams, almost every day; after that touch. It's like God installed something inside of me. When I asked around about the touch, people would begin to tell me that I had an out of body experience. In which, as long as it was God and not something else evil trying to grab me and touch on me, I was fine with that.

    The dream that I had the night that I felt the touch, referred to one of my favorite aunts "Ruby," whom was really sick with cancer. She did pass away the day after the dream but a couple of weeks before she passed away, the strangest thing had taken place, while I was at the hospital with her daughters. I decided to grab my aunt's feet and began to pray for her, when suddenly all the lights in the hospital and the backup generators shut down at once. The hospital was now in total darkness and the employees could not figure out what happened. They explained to us that they had never dealt with anything like this before. One of my favorite cousins Tammy, which is my aunt's oldest daughter looked at me and said, "Wow, Antwan you are so powerful!" This Christian journey was new to me so I told her that it must have been God answering my

THE TOTALITY OF DELIVERANCE

prayers. Within six hours they were moving my aunt to another hospital that they had referred her to; for hospice care. She then desired to go to her own home, in which the dream that I had was everything that we were doing, as far as taking her home and moving her to another bed. Also, we were making her surroundings peaceful and comfortable at home. The next day when she passed away, had kind of affected me in a major way. I could not really focus at school but yet I still pressed on. It was rough for me to go to school all day and still go to church heavily, while doing hair on the side to pay for my living expenses. After all, I really needed to do all of them in order for my life to stay on course. I needed to stay at church to help keep my sanity with this life changing experience and I definitely had to stay in school in order to keep doing hair the legal way, to pay my bills. Well, my other favorite cousin Faye would let me come over and work at her daycare for a few hours. It was not many because of my school schedule, but it did help out a lot.

Attending school became very challenging because there were so many non-believers, that it begun to hurt my spirit man. Mainly because there were so many lost souls that were there in my presence. I then begin to witness to them at school while I was also witnessing to my family, friends and my clients at home. I would begin by asking all of them this direct question, "What do you

THE TOTALITY OF DELIVERANCE

think about Jesus?" Many of their answers were so rude and disappointing that I probably would never repeat most of them to anyone. Let alone in this book. Next, I would begin to tell them all about Jesus and how he had come into my life and changed every part of me. Most of them agreed that something had changed in me or that they have noticed there was something different about me. I noticed that many of them were listening to me and taking in my testimony, as well as beginning to dwell on God more. This would start a whole new vision for my life! I would go around and tell people, young and old all of the good things that Jesus Christ has done for me, now that I have surrendered my life unto God. I then made a deal with God, I asked him to send me the clients to witness to and I would send them back to him. I felt like he agreed to the deal, because my clientele increased greatly. Many of the clients needed to know about Jesus Christ, or learn how to know him on a more personal level and some even needed to be baptized or restored.

I graduated from cosmetology school and began to work in a huge salon where I brought many of my clients. There, I shouted around and extremely witnessed to them all. I then began to feel like the atmosphere of the salon was hindering my witness to the clients. Just because I felt that it was ok for them to come to a salon where they are learning about Jesus Christ. Moreover, their souls were

THE TOTALITY OF DELIVERANCE

more important to me than their total salon visit. Referring, more to the worldly music, the foul language, the fights, the arguments and all of the ungodly events that not only took place at this beauty salon but at most beauty salons. About one year later the lord made a way for me to open up my own beauty salon. In which he had given me the name for it while I was in my prayer closet. He told me to name it "Holy Hands." Within 6 months I had already out grown this little beauty salon. The lord had increased my hair skills as well as my clientele. At this time I was winning many of souls to Jesus Christ, just by the testimony of my life and the things that the people around me witness God do for me. I would witness to them and invite them to church and they would come and receive the baptism of the Lord Jesus Christ, with many of them leaving with the evidence of speaking in other tongues. In which, there would be a minister that would meet us there at church even if it was not on a Sunday morning service, which was normally "Minister Simpson (Scooter)." I even had my mother, my brother, my sister and her son Tahvone baptized in the name of the Lord Jesus Christ. This baptism did open all of us up to a new revelation of Jesus Christ. Tahvone is ten years of age and recognized the difference after this baptism. I recognized this because after the baptism he started telling us things that he began to see and deal with in dreams and in the

THE TOTALITY OF DELIVERANCE

natural. Tahvone is my nephew that I love so dear, because he gives me a little feeling of how I would feel if I had a son. Mainly because he looks like me and was my only blood related nephew for a very long time.

  I then moved again into another apartment, but this time I moved very far from the areas where I usually would live. Due to the break in's that had occurred at the old apartments. I had lived in that apartment complex for a total of nine years before I moved. The last burglary was so bad that I wondered if God was sleep and what did I do wrong for something like this to happen to me? They destroyed my home at once and nearly left me with the mindset that it was time to relocate and never ever to return to my own home again. I prayed and prayed for answers and yes, God did give me answers. They destroyed my home so bad that the police called in special people to come and do finger printing, picture taking, and they even asked the neighbors as well as threatened the maintenance men at the apartments. Not only did they take pictures but I did too, and there was something very strange about the last two pictures that I had taken. The Holy Spirit spoke to me and told me to review the pictures again and again. Then I noticed that there were two faces in the pictures that were not in the room where they were taken. One of the faces was an evil face with a shady smile and the other face, was facing towards that face, with tall crowns on his head. I took the camera to a few preachers and they told me whatever the Holy Spirit said to me, that's what it is because they agreed on recognizing the faces as well. What the Holy Spirit was saying to me about the faces was that, God allowed the enemy to break-in but it was for my own good. It was to provide a way for me to get out of those apartments. I then remembered that all things happen for a reason and they do work together for the good of those who love the Lord.

A few days later, God did give me a dream that revealed to me who had broken into my home. It was too late because the officers had the office to notify the owner of the apartments, which came right away. Moreover, the owner then released me from my lease. In which, I had been praying hard to move far from there because it held too many memories from my past and too many old friends knew where I lived. This was a hinder to me because old friends would stop by no matter what time of day or night it was. I must say, after they came in and I told them how God had changed my life, they really didn't stop by anymore. Besides they had stopped coming around me as much because they were into other things and drugs that I was not into. Drugs like powder or cocaine, which was not a drug of my choice or any drug at this present point and time in my life. I then moved to an unfamiliar side of the city, where I had a new beginning

THE TOTALITY OF DELIVERANCE

and no visitors at all. In fact, I moved too far for most people that I had known, to just travel on a hum bug. Indeed it was God reconstructing my life and meeting my desires all at once.

At the beginning of every year I would always commit my first forty days to fasting unto the Lord. During this fast, God would normally surprise me by revealing family members on my father side of the family, whom I never knew or did not have any contact with. Being my father did pass away while I was still young, without introducing me unto many of his family members. The year I moved to the other side of town, I met my favorite cousin Dominic Amey who introduced me to other relatives that I did not know that lived here in Indiana. The following year the Lord would have my brother Teo Amey to regain contact with me via Face Book, along with my sister Mici and my brother Eric that also resides in the same state where Teo lives. I did not know much about them nor have I ever met them in person, but I did speak to each of them one time, twelve years ago and then we lost contact. Later on that year, I discovered another brother Tre and sister Tierney that lives in a different state from them. Meeting my relatives on my father side really inspired me because this was a part of me that was missing that I wanted, so bad.

Part 4

(Early Thirties)

Freedom ~ Set Free ~ New Character

Now that I have grown in the spirit, I also have out grown the salon that I was working in. The LORD would move me into a new salon in which, I then recognized that it was my ministry, "HOLY HANDS." It was then when I began to meet all types of preachers, some were even prophets of God. I can remember one interesting night when I was with my aunt Sheila, my cousin Tammy and my friend Adrian, when we had gone to a service to hear a preacher that came to our city to preach. He was a well, known prophet that would come on a gospel station on the radio every day. I remember listening to him on a daily basis as he preached and taught in a way where even a baby could understand it. I was not familiar with how prophecy worked neither have I ever been in the presence of a prophet while knowing that it was his calling. As we were sitting there listening to him preach and teach he began to prophesize to a few of the members of the congregation. That's when he walked up to my aunt Sheila and looked her in the face and then he looked at my

THE TOTALITY OF DELIVERANCE

cousin Tammy in the face, next he looked at me and lastly he looked at my friend Adrian and looked back at me and asked, "are you connected to somebody name Antwan?" In which this was really amusing to me because I had never seen this man before, in fact he wasn't even from Indiana but he knew my name. I responded and said, "I am Antwan!" He then asked me to stand up and come to the front with him. He told the congregation that the glory of God was all over this man, in which I had never heard anyone tell somebody this before. He began to prophesy to me, but lastly he told me that my hands were anointed and that everything that they touch is blessed. Next, he asked one of his armor bearers to get his oil and give it to him. That's when he put some oil on my hands and then touched me and I instantly collapsed. It's like I had lost total control of my body and blanked out, but when I looked back up I could only see people reaching for my hands, while listening to my aunt Sheila screaming and praising God. On the way home I had my friend Adrian with me that was there also. We were both so stunned that God had done something so amazing like this all we could do was cry.

When I woke up the next day, I was still in shock from the prophetic word that I had received and all of the details that the man of God had spoken over my life. I still could not believe that he even called out the ministry that was to come forth in my life, in the near future.

My friend Adrian that was with me was a younger guy that I met at church. He had just become a member at Mt. Zion when our "Sr. Executive Associate Pastor Stone," a very sweet woman of God came to me one Sunday while Adrian was at the altar. She took his hand and put it in my hand and told Adrian to stick with me and told me to hang on to him. God had already informed me earlier that day, this was going to happen. For just about two and a half years Adrian was there with me, when God began the ultimate transitional stages of my life; as far as new gifts and spiritual insight. He received a lot of insight on what God was doing with me but he was not the only one because there were other roommates who had lived with me and received spiritual insight, on what God was doing with me; but it did not work out. When they would come and stay with me, they would bring other spirits with them that would cause me to slip and fall and miss the mark at times. I can remember a time when one of my roommates came and got in the bed with me, which was ok because we had never touched each other. But this particular night his body was touching mines in a strange way and it felt as if a magnet was pulling us together. As if another spirit had come inside my room and made us perform as if we were not on a journey with Jesus. The next day when we got into my car I slid on a little bitty piece of ice and hit a brick wall that totaled my car. I knew exactly what this meant. It was a sign that I had made a big mistake that would cost me in the long run and that I needed to be very cautious about who I let sleep in my bed. Besides I've had almost forty cars and only been in one car accident, where another car crossed the street without looking both ways; he was at fault. This was a lesson well learned! Then there was my newest best friend Tony, whom I did know from the lifestyle before this. We were also on the Christian journey together but he had his own home because he was well older than me. It would take someone to be around me 24/7 to watch how God worked miraculously towards my life daily. Tony did witness God's hand move upon my life with great power.

That prophecy that I received, made me desire even more of God, so much that all I was doing was eating, singing and dreaming Jesus. I began to understand what Jesus was referring to, when he quoted in the Holy Bible, "The harvest is plentiful but the laborers were few (Matthew 9:37)." It was beginning to feel like no one understood my love for Jesus Christ or why I was so radical for him. Most of them still insist on pressuring me about my love for Christ, by telling me that it does not take all of that and that God is nothing new. Geesh! This had gotten to me, because I was a hairstylist that got a chance to be one on one with all kinds of people with many opinions. That did lead me to another approach. I began to ask them "can I pray for them? What did they know about Jesus? Or what have they learned about God period?" I started to ask them all, "have you not only, been baptized in Jesus name, but also baptized with the Holy Spirit?" I also asked them, "do they speak in other tongues and is there anybody on this earth that they love more than King Jesus?" I began this questioning while I was working at a barber shop, because I had out grown the last beauty salon I was in. God then made a way for me to get a salon room of my own, within a salon, which was one of my favorite cousin's, Michelle. She asked me to be the manager of her salon, at the same time that I was working in my own salon, in the same building. God had stepped in and gave me a spot where I would shout around, listening to gospel music, preaching, teaching and doing hair at the same time. I believe this made a great impact on not only the area the salon was located but also on the many of souls that came through the door. In return the Lord God was giving me the victory over many, to win their souls to Christ! The salon was a blessing because it was more than just a regular church ministry to me. Besides, God had given me the name "Holy Hands" so I took it as a privilege and ran with it, just because he gave it to me. In return I would use it for his glory and to bring fame to his name. As well as, using this gift and talent to make money to survive with.

I did participate in many of hair shows, during the last salon that I worked in and also hair shows in cosmetology school too. I also entered into many of hair shows years before that, with my aunt Sheila. Then there was a category in the Ball Scene that was called "Hair Affair," that I would enter into and win as well. My aunt Sheila worked with a well, known product company that I would sometimes help out at the bigger hair shows in state and out of state. So, I was kind of done doing the hair shows but I did enter into a few newspapers and magazines and really that was enough for me. After all it was not hard getting clients, because God would send the ones that he wanted me to witness to.

The salon last about one year, but in the middle of the year I desired to go higher in God. I began to do more like, attend prophetic seminars and different religious seminars in other states. In which I learned how to use my prophetic gift more fluently. By this time I was hearing from God more than just in my closet. Moreover, I was referring to myself as an" Ambassador for Christ," because every time I would come around someone, they would start saying, "here comes the Ambassador, Rev, Bishop or Preacher man." It did not bother me, besides I felt it was

THE TOTALITY OF DELIVERANCE

ok because the bible speaks about everyone being an Ambassador. Besides the only thing that I talked about and really cared about was Jesus; because I was so infatuated with him and his amazing grace upon my life. Although, I really did not have a title, neither was I looking for one. Besides, I come from a Baptist church where we were only familiar with Reverends. On the night just before my birthday, January 30, 2014, while I was in my prayer room, God told me that I was an Apostle and to go change my name on Face Book to "Apostle For Christ Antwan Amey." Either I was being elevated in God or he was letting me know exactly who and what I was. Then there were many of preachers and prophets that I did not know, who would confirm the Apostle calling upon my life. In which that was good news to me because I desire to go higher and higher in God but not by labeling, but spiritually. I then knew that I was growing spiritually. In my prayer room was a "Tallit" or "Prayer Shawl," that I had ordered a few years back, off of a television show that had a program about it. Following the program they made an offer to order one by sewing a seed into that ministry. The Holy Spirit nudged me to get it, without me knowing what I would do with it later on down the road. God would have a prophet to call my phone and tell me to add a garment with the colors of pure white, royal blue and sky blue to my daily apparel. I was puzzled for a minute then the Holy

THE TOTALITY OF DELIVERANCE

Spirit brought it to my mind that he was referring to the tallit in my prayer closet. In which, I was obedient because I did not know the man and he could have not known that I had the tallit with those colors on it. Besides, I never told anyone about it nor did anyone ever enter into my prayer room. Of course I verified this with God first, because I felt this was something out of my league and very strange as well. God told me to wear it and do not take it off because it was my covering and also another form of witnessing to the world. It definitely got a lot of attention because I wear it to church, the malls and most everywhere I go. Whenever I wear it, there is always someone who stops me and questions me about it. Believe it or not, it really does help to open up their eyes to God and our Lord and Savior Jesus Christ; once I explain the shawl and its purpose to them. It took a lot of getting used to wearing it everywhere I go, because of the fringes on it but that's the main part of why God instructed me to wear it. Also, the Shawl helps me to remember the commandments that I live out now through Christ Jesus. I notice, without this tallit on things are different and I don't feel the same way as I do when it is on. The Tallit has become a part of more than my apparel but a shaper of my character, because it keeps me in memory of Christ Jesus. Needless to say, that God was moving on his time of elevation and at his speed, being he is the one who promotes and elevates us to the next level in him.

I then begin to prepare myself because I was told that a new level brings with it a new devil, and yes the heat was on. I had to fight a lot of different things in my dreams but this next level was not too surprising, because of the past experience of weird things and dreams that I will never forget. God had spoken to me one day and told me that I was like Joshua, in the Holy Bible. He told me that I was one of his mighty warriors and that is how I feel. Mainly because, I'm always praying or fighting in my dreams and in the spirit realm for other people a lot.

Within, three months left before this salon will close, I would begin to deal with the death of my grandmother Luvenia Kilpatrick. She was whom I had loved so dear. I always dreaded this day since my very child hood. I can remember telling myself, that when my grandmother passed away and left here I was going to kill myself and leave with her as well. I meant that so much that it stuck with me throughout my lifetime. To where it became one of my biggest pet peeves, just to imagine her in a casket. I can also remember asking God to please let her live until I make it to at least the age of twenty-five. God had done this for me and actually he allowed me to make it to the age of thirty-one at the time of her passing

THE TOTALITY OF DELIVERANCE

away. In which she got a chance to witness God changing my life before she left the earth. I had decided to change my life and give it to God at the end of the year in 2008. I was twenty-six years of age when I started it but twenty-seven when things began to come together for me. Eight months before my grandmother passed away, when I was in my prayer closet, God asked me; "would you stop loving me if I took your grandmother away?" I told him, "of course not!" He responded by saying, "good because I am about to remove her from that place!" He began to give me details on what date she was going to pass away and even the time. He told me what color to put her in and that I was going to be responsible for this occasion and in charge of my family. I then came out of the closet in despair saying, "What did I just hear? I cannot believe this, maybe I am just tripping? Maybe I'm just talking to myself?" No it was correct, because the next day when I stopped at a store not too far from my grandmother's house, I bumped into my favorite uncle Robert. He was my grandmother's care giver that lived with her. He smiled at me and gave me a hug and told me that he and my grandmother had decided to put me in charge of her funeral. He did not know that God had already informed me of everything, the night before I bumped into him at the store. Actually, it was God who put me in charge because I already had everything written down on paper

THE TOTALITY OF DELIVERANCE

and how things were going to go; according to God. I had butterflies in my stomach for months in secret mourning. I was so nervous but God instructed me to wait until after the funeral to mourn privately at home.

My roommate Adrian had moved out just in time; which was good because I was going to need the space to deal with this alone, just me and God. I can remember the count down until it happen. Things had gotten a little rocky, meaning we had family fallouts, huge debates, arguments over material things and who's in charge. I personally felt she was mistreated, just because of who she was, to all of us. I can remember a time when I went to visit her and as I walked in, my favorite aunt, Jean approached me, trying to convince me that she was going to make a cd and that my favorite cousin Tyrie Rudolph, who is a well-known beautiful model was not the only family member that was going to be in the spotlight. I began to prophesy to her as I begin to feel the spirit, because I did not recognize that she was really serious. I then went into the kitchen where I saw my grandmother looking down and out trying to find something to cook, but there was really nothing in the house that was a complete meal. I then told her that I didn't have any food and that I had just left from over my favorite aunt, Darlene's house; who really didn't have a complete meal either. I then noticed that something was wrong with her.

THE TOTALITY OF DELIVERANCE

So, I asked her and she told me that she did not have any money and that her medicine was all gone. Also, she still owed some money for the last medicine she had gotten. I pulled out my wallet and counted my money; I had just enough to help her out. She was so happy and pleased with me; her smile was so big it made me smile. She then told me that she knew that the Lord would make away somehow, and I told her that I definitely agreed with that.

    Many of my friends and clients that has large families and have already dealt with losing the "rock" of their family. Told me that our family would fall apart, but I didn't believe them. I believe that it was just a part of the grieving process. However, with God being in control everything worked out and we managed to get on through it. In fact, a few months after the funeral, God had given me a dream, informing me that my grandmother did make it home safely. Not to mention, our family still remain to show our love for each other, so much that we even continue to have our annual pitch in for Thanksgiving and other holidays. Although, I love every one of my family members and as you can see they are all my favorites. Life is still so different without the rock of the family being here, but I must continue to go higher in God. I truly believe that this new walk with God is the only reason why I was able to handle this season of my life. After losing my father, my grandfather, and the other family members

THE TOTALITY OF DELIVERANCE

that has gone on and left me, I have come to an understanding that we all have to leave here by way of death and the grave. Although, it will hurt for a little while and maybe even a little distraught at times I must continue on living my life's journey. I will forever miss my grandmother, and the other family members. Yet, I am ok with them leaving here being God is the total source of my life. In which, I found this out the first time I was deeply hurt, burdened and distraught, when my father passed away. God then informed me that he would be with me and that he would never leave me. The Holy Bible teaches us to be absent in the body is to be present with the Lord (2Corinthians 5:8). God has always been the father that I never had as well as my grandfather when he passed away. Now, that I look back, he was always there for me in every situation, no matter what or who it was. He might not have come, when I wanted him to but he was there right on time; every time. God has always filled in the void that I felt from not only missing my father's love but also anything else that I lacked in my life. Even if it was not recognizable, I knew it and felt him working on my behalf.

When coming through the grieving process it really helps to know, that the Lord gives and the Lord takes away; which makes it hard to grieve for long when knowing the potter abstracted his clay. I didn't need to pretty much worry about where my father and the other

THE TOTALITY OF DELIVERANCE

family members were at, or even their total death at all because I knew that they believed in Jesus and was present with the Lord. I always feel like, God prepares me for the things that are going to happen to me by surprise and he always guides my mind and spirit during the time of all despair.

    Within just three weeks of the salon being closed, one of my best friends and I went on a trip to New York. I was going to a prophetic seminar and he was just visiting the city for the first time. On the first day, the seminar was extremely different and strange because most of the people that were there had on brown hooded robes. When I first seen them I was nerves and was thinking to myself, "so is this some kind of occult or something?" But really I was kind of asking God indirectly, what's going on here? Then the next day when we arrived all together, in the big meeting room, they began to prophesy to each other, about two to three hundred different people. I did get in line and received some prophecies myself. Some of them were correct or on point but others were wrong and way off. I then asked God, "What is this?" He responded by saying, "even my very elect!" In which, is a quote out of the Holy Bible, that refers to the true prophets of God that are under a misleading leadership. I knew from that point forward what he was saying. But he used it as a tool to sharpen up my prophetic gifting. Needless to say, that I

THE TOTALITY OF DELIVERANCE

was really ready to go but I had two more days left of this foolishness. It really wasn't all that bad! It was real prophets that were there, they were just under the wrong leadership. I too can hear clear and very clear from God but they must remember another voice we shall not follow. After speaking with and receiving prophesies from almost 200 to 300 people, there I learned one of my greatest lessons, which was to discern the real from the fake.

As, my best friend and I, arrived back to the airport to prepare for departure, we found out that our flight was delayed because of bad weather. I can remember praying very hard in that airport telling the Lord that I cannot stay another night in this city. They decided to let us leave about 45 minutes later, in which made our connector flight in the other city 45 minutes late also; being they held it for us. Right before we arrived to the connector flight, the flight attendant made the announcement that we needed to get to the trolley as fast as we could. Being, the plane has been sitting there waiting with people on board just for us. When we had land, I jumped up and ran out of the plane towards the wrong gate. I noticed that I was in the wrong place and then turned around and caught up with everyone else and jumped on the trolley with them. I was running like I was in a race. Then I noticed that the trolley was leaving without my best friend

THE TOTALITY OF DELIVERANCE

aboard. So, I asked the driver to hold on for a minute because my brother was not on board yet and that he was on the same plane that we were all on. He told me that he could not wait because they had dispatched him to pull off and drop us off at the plane but he did promise me that he would bring him right back. As we approached the plane and the woman collected my ticket, I told her that my brother was left by the trolley and that he was on his way back with him. She said, "Ok" and I proceeded on to the plane where I noticed a guy in a pilot's uniform. I then told him the same thing and he said that he probably would be safe to make it before we had left. By this time I looked out of the window and I saw my best friend on the trolley coming over to the plane, but when he got off of the trolley and came up all of those stairs, he turned the wrong way when he walked into the building. I noticed that they had moved the stairs out of the way then they cut the lights off on the inside of the plane, as we began to roll backwards. I could not believe what was going on, so I looked at the guy dressed like a pilot and said "I thought you were the pilot?" He told me that he was a pilot, just not the pilot of this plane and then sat down in front of me. As we were pulling back, I could see my best friend approaching the gate attendant but it was already too late and there was nothing I could do. He could not get on the plane and I could not get off. As, we began to get higher and higher into the sky and into the clouds, I was looking at him, as he got smaller and smaller. God began to speak to me. He said "do you see what just happen and how you caught the flight and he was left there?" He then told me if anyone of my friends, do not change their life like I did and serve him, this is exactly what is going to happen to them when he returns! Basically he told me to tell them don't miss their flight!

    Now with the salon closing God would have me to go to the different nursing homes doing hair with my favorite cousin Angie and my aunt Sheila. There I would pray with the residents and uplift their spirits. Until he gives me my next assignment, in which God told me that he was preparing me for a Deliverance Ministry. I gave a commitment to God to totally live as a witness of the Lord Jesus Christ as I continue to win souls for him daily and to build up the Kingdom of God for the rest of my days here on earth. I really love my new life with Jesus Christ, who is the best thing that ever happened to me.

This is just a brief over view of my life story perhaps in the near future a more in-depth over view is possible. May God Bless You!

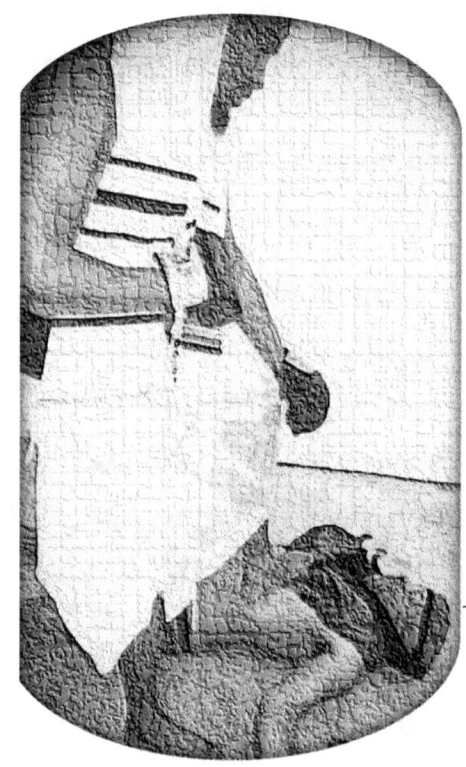

The Phases Of Total Deliverance

THE TOTALITY OF DELIVERANCE

Deliverance

Deliverance (Noun) 1.) The action of being rescued or set Free.
Synonyms: liberation, release, delivery discharge, Rescue, Emancipation, salvation; bailout

2.) A formal or authoritative utterance.
Synonyms: utterance, statement, announcement, pronouncement, declaration, proclamation, lecture, speech

To really obtain deliverance when coming out of homosexuality one must first began to claim it. Notice the first part of the definition is to show action. That means beginning to act as if it was already done; showing freedom or acting released. (Reference the synonyms as well.) Then take a look at the second meaning, in which it's basically opening your mouth and decreeing this freedom and announcing it as well as proclaiming it. Remember that the Bible teaches us to speak those things into existence, although they are not yet (Romans 4:17). When you claim it you can obtain it. You must believe that you are delivered and not just in your mind, body, heart

THE TOTALITY OF DELIVERANCE

and soul but your spirit man must know that you are feeling this way. Also, your spiritual ears must hear you proclaim it, so he could obtain it and act upon it as well. All the while, you are already showing it and calling the new man forth into existence. That means praising God for bringing you out, as well as hanging with others who have been delivered or brought out of similar lifestyles. Do not take any actions in any of the practices of the lifestyle or whatever it is that you desire God to deliver you from. Then the God of all grace will give you the desires of your heart, because you are seeking him and his will for your life. One must look to God for this to happen, because you must first download into your mind, heart, soul and spirit that deliverance is what I need, in order to walk as a true man or woman of God. As a mighty man of valor or a woman of virtue, along with your integrity would make it even easier, "to come boldly to the throne of grace!" Nevertheless, the most important part of the deliverance aspect, is to shut the doors of the strong holds. As well as, all of the discriminative acts that played a part in the lifestyle or the issue that you are being delivered from. One must continue to keep these doors shut and closed at all times because once that door is cracked the enemy will use that crack to try and kick the door open with heavy force. You must continue to strategize on how you are going to avoid, re-opening these doors. Your conscience or the voice of God can really help dictate this situation firmly. Make sure that you are listening to your inner man or gut feeling, in which is actually your Holy Spirit. Your Holy Spirit will give you warning signs, that the activity or

THE TOTALITY OF DELIVERANCE

situation that you are about to indulge in, may crack open one of the closed doors. Some examples of things to watch for are phone conversations, certain places, certain people, certain music, certain movies or television shows, certain sites on the world-wide-web, certain friend request on social media and the wrong trip down memory lane. Remember, to keep your mind stayed on Jesus throughout the whole deliverance process which would allow you to download the things and nature of God. Keeping your mind stayed on Jesus will make the deliverance process a more fulfilling and joyful experience. If not the enemy will try to steal this time and use it against your joy, peace and happiness. Once you've received your deliverance, you must fight to keep it. Meaning you must do the things that delivered people do and that is give God the praise, talk about where he has brought you from and proclaim Christianity, so that your mind will not slip into the old way of thinking. You must understand that you will have the anointing to help others to get to their deliverance because the blood of the lamb and the word of our testimony is how we overcome (Revelation 12:11).

Freedom

The first part of being free from anything is to learn how to let go of whatever it is. With the mindset and the understanding, that this would not; only be the best option, but the only choice for this particular situation. Even if it means to let it go just for this season in your life, for a few years, or maybe just letting it go forever. Letting it go with the intentions that this is not for my good any longer, specifically if it's not in God's plans or will, for your life. If you hold on to something that is not meant for you, it would only hinder you from God's best for your life. In the Homosexual lifestyle this would be one of the first understandings that your mind would need to perceive, in order for the process to begin to take place. When I first begun this new change of life, I had to download this very thing into my mind. I then came to an understanding, that this lifestyle is not what God desires for my life. First, I had to research on what I was created for. Next, I had to line everything up with God's word and the things that does not line up with his word, must soon be discarded from my life. That it would all line up with his plans and make my life more enjoyable to live. Without lining your life up properly with God's plans for your life, you will continue to live a life that is not fulfilling, not enjoyable and definitely not successful. The reason why the God factor has to be immediately considered in the freedom section of the total deliverance process is, because without God and the cross you would have never been set free. Also, you would have never set your mind on Christ coming and shedding his blood for your freedom, as well as your restoration.

To me, I believe that freedom is a mindset that you must have faith in and then live out what you believe. Which means I'm no longer set in the mind frame that I am living a lifestyle that, not only the real world disagrees with but also a lifestyle that God considers to be an abomination. This would mean that God is not pleased with this part of my life and if there's anything that God is not pleased with, that means this is an issue that needs to be handled immediately. If not handled immediately, life's difficulties and hinders will not stop. On top of that, I understand how God deals with abominations, in which includes the homosexual and lesbian life style. The Holy Bible informs us in Romans 1 that they became vain in their imaginations and their foolish hearts was darkened. (Romans 1:21) That they were professing themselves to be wise but they became fools. (Romans 1:22) Next God gave them up to uncleanness through the lusts of their own hearts to dishonor their own bodies between themselves.

THE TOTALITY OF DELIVERANCE

(Romans 1:24) Also, for this cause God gave them up unto vile passions and a reprobate mind. Not only that, but the bible states that at the end of their lives, they will receive the penalty for their error, which was due (Death). The Bible refers to the grave as sleep and death as eternal damnation or Hell. When I read this and downloaded it into my heart and recollect on it for a little while. I came to the understanding that if I'm not trying to go to hell, then I can't live this kind of lifestyle and go to heaven. My next thought was to figure out how do I, obtain this major life change without losing my mind. Being, homosexuality is a way of life, that means I would have to change my way of thinking, the way I live, the people I'm around, my total environment and my total way of even existing in life. It would mean starting a new life all over again. Depending on how long we were grounded into the lifestyle. As well as, how long all of the aspects that we are changing in our lives, has been downloaded into our mind, our system, our talk, our walk, our actions, even our heart and our total swag.

In which, this lifestyle is really an illusion from Satan, and so was the way that I had carried myself, as an illusion too. No, I was not a drag queen but I was not a man of valor that God had created me to be. Which means my current lifestyle was not what God had desired for my life. So, once again it's not going to fit me, look good on me and

THE TOTALITY OF DELIVERANCE

it's not going to work out, because God says no and my soul says yes to God. When you are trying to do well or good, God will then turn the situation around, which means you will begin to live right. You will begin to recognize the wrong from the right, while some things you have to live them out to find out that they do not work on this journey, like sin. Sin will not work on this journey for long, it may feel right and it might even appear to be ok. You may even get a lot of people who agree with you, but if it is sin you can count on it pulling you down and causing you to miss the mark every time. You must turn from all kinds of sin because sin soon leads to death and there is no other way around it. That's also in the word of God and the word will stand (Romans 6:23). Sometimes God has to let his children go through the chastening process or even punishment training, to wake them up to do the right thing. Not to mention, anything that you do wrong, when you are called to do something by God will affect the process. Sort of like the story in the Holy Bible starring "Jonah and the big fish." When you are called to do the works of the Lord, most of the time people say, "It's a choice that you make," but I believe that it really isn't. If you do not do what God has called you to do your life will mean nothing and I mean completely nothing as well as a miserable state of mind. Keep in mind your salvation is then in jeopardy because you really have not been doing

THE TOTALITY OF DELIVERANCE

what the creator has created you to do. It is not healthy to live your life in total disobedience to God. Visually, I see living your life in complete disobedience, as you being out on a limb over a cliff of brimstone and fire, without you wanting to receive help from anyone, specifically not God. In which that is nothing but a trap of the enemy, whispering lies in your ear, putting fear in your heart or whatever it is that is keeping you from following God's will for your life.

 With that being said, you must find out what God desires for your life and that will began by reading, studying and researching the Holy Bible. The Holy Bible is the basic instructions for the proper way to serve and live on earth as well as the connection to God through the Holy Spirit and through Jesus Christ teachings. Also, you have to focus on becoming wise, because the bible teaches us to pray for wisdom as well as wisdom is the beginning to fearing the Lord(Psalms 111:10). Until we comprehend, that this is God's world and that he made the planet that we live on. In which, this is why he is the creator of not only people, but everything that we see and don't see. Everything must go the way that God has planned for it to go or the way he designed it to be or it may be in great jeopardy of not even existing anymore. Being he made us out of dirt, he can send us right back to dirt and our souls to eternal damnation and after all it is better to be than not to be. It

THE TOTALITY OF DELIVERANCE

would definitely be a great benefit for us to reside in heaven with God, once we have left this earth. For me I fear God and make it a great point to get Godly counsel for my life each and every day. Rather if it's from, reading my Holy Bible, going to church on a weekly basis, praying and meditating, communicating with God, watching the preachers on television, or rewinding the things from my past that I would make great mistakes on, so that I would not make them again. Ultimately it is Faith that pleases God and Faith comes by hearing the word of God (Romans 10:17). Now that God has opened my eyes to the real world and yes I said, "open my eyes" because I had lived a blind man's lifestyle and could not see what I was doing. I now understand the things of the spirit because God is a spirit and everyone that worships him must do it in spirit and in truth (John 4:24).

    Jesus, from the biblical stand point is truth, in which we must worship God in the spirit through Jesus Christ. Finally, you must have your eyes open by Jesus spiritually to understand the things of the spirit. Once Jesus has opened up your eyes to understand the things of the spirit, you will then realize who you are and who's, you are. It is then, when you will be able to walk in abundance of freedom and will be able to proclaim that, "I am free, free, free at last!"

THE TOTALITY OF DELIVERANCE

Darken Heart

If your heart is darkened, the things that you deal with in your life will be viewed and handled in the way that the kingdom of darkness would handle it (Satan's Kingdom). Because in God there is no darkness (1John1:5) (Colossians 1:13). Which means things will be deceiving you, darkening your emotions and your life's duties will not really be constructive. In fact, you won't be able to carry out anything, according to the "Father Of Lights, (God's)" kingdom's mannerism. In which we knew that he has called us to be the light of the world (Matthew 5:14). Your life will be hard to cope with because you cannot see clearly. The Holy Bible, states that out of the Heart flows the issues of life (Proverbs 4:23). Love is also flowing through the heart, right along with the attacks of life that is triggered from the mind, which is our battlefield (Romans 12:2), (2Corinthians 10:5). Being that life is in the blood which circulates through the heart, the heart determines the blood flow from the way that we deal with life's issues. This is the reason why we immediately check for a heartbeat, when we are verifying that someone is still alive or have been severely injured, because your

THE TOTALITY OF DELIVERANCE

body cannot operate correctly without the proper heartbeat or heart rate. In which, the heart plays the roll, of the body's total function. When the God that created you has allowed your heart to become totally darkened, this means everything that you deal with personally will be dark. Including, the way you think, the way you perceive things, the way you talk, the way you obey, the way you believe, the things that you love and the way that you love. The total operation of your life will be dark, meaning you will see things from a worldly type of view. Being the world has been darkened and manipulated by Satan and his kingdom of darkness; which is a well-known fact. For the Homosexuals and Lesbians, the Bible states that the first thing that happens to this nature of sin is that they become vain in their imaginations and their foolish hearts are darkened (Romans 1:21). I am a witness to that because anytime that I had to deal with something in my lifetime, before I changed my life and gave it to God, I would react upon it according to what felt better to me and not following or obeying God's input on it. This darkening of the heart allows you to understand and to believe wrongly, by allowing you to feel that you were born to live in this lifestyle. It also allows you to believe that the Holy Bible made a mistake, when it came to what it said about living in this homosexual lifestyle. This lifestyle of sin, even causes you to come to turns to, who

THE TOTALITY OF DELIVERANCE

and what you really are. The heart is so darkened that you cannot see the light side of view, for the sins that are being committed in your life. The darkening of the heart prevents you from recognizing Jesus Christ, for all of the reasons why he came down to earth, as well as God's point of view on our sins. In which, one must carefully fast and pray for God to lighten or remove the darkness from your heart. Remember to keep in mind that in God there is no darkness (1John 1:5). Also, with Jesus being the light and God in flesh we need to understand God's point of view and rules, as well as the consequences for sin. I personally believe that we are living in the darkest of ages, to where the things that are wrong are considered right and the way of righteousness is wrong. I also believe that we have fallen away from God's Holy word, because the Holy Bible informs us that his word is a lamp unto my feet (Psalms119:105), and I don't see too many people living off of his Holy word. Or too many people footsteps, that appear to be ordered by the Lord. This is the reason why the world is experiencing so much difficulty and bloodshed. As well as, the result of the darkness that is in the world, causing the confusion for the way of truth. In which, God is not the author of confusion Satan is. I believe, this insist that we need to get back to reading God's Holy Word and we also need to allow our hearts to be led by the Holy Spirit.

Vile Passions

Vile-Disgustingly or utterly bad or morally despicable;
Passion- A strong liking or desire for or to some Activity,
Object, or Sexual Desire;

Vile Passions means a strong desire for disgusting sex or morally despicable activity. Once we have put the meaning of the two words together in reference to the Holy Bible. Vile Passions is the next thing that God gives the Homosexuals and lesbians over to after he has allowed them to receive a darkened heart (Romans 1:26). Keep in mind that he is our creator and if the creator gives you over to something, surely you are going to do it. Mainly, because it was something that you had in your heart and mind that you were trying so strongly to do. Vile Passion is the part of you that makes you feel like you are so deeply in love with the wrong person, place or thing. I found out personally that it's the part of you that touches the heart, the mind, the body and the soul. This is a very important part because it makes you feel like you are meant for that person and they were meant for you; when really it's all a big deception. The way that you desire to have sex, after

THE TOTALITY OF DELIVERANCE

God has given you over to vile passions, is disgustingly, despicable and it is forbidden in his eyes. It is a big set up to mess you up and to help your life to succeed in total disaster. Just think about how two people of the same sex have to perform in order to have sex. Some even have to use other items that are not even considered sexual parts or parts of the human body; like toys, fake parts and battery operated items etc. Now, that connects back to a darkened heart; referring to you not even knowing why you are having sex. To have sex without using sexual parts or to use other parts of the body that are not affiliated with the parts that were created to have sex with, is verification that you are in a delusional state of mind. That's like using your ankles to clap with and not your hands or using your knees to smell with instead of your nose. Those parts, were not created to be used in that manner and God did not intend for it to be that a way. To feel like you have made love, after having sex in such manner, is an indication to me of a "Soul Tie." In which my understanding of a "Soul Tie" is when two have connected together in the spirit sexually but in a bad way if you are not married. This can be prayed off of the person and depending on the situation most times fasting is needed. Remember that sex is a gift to the marriage bed, so if you are not married you shouldn't be eligible to have sex, according to God's Holy word (Hebrew 13:4), whom is our creator. As well as, the Holy Bible stating over and over along with its examples, throughout the whole entire bible that marriage is between a man and a woman. Same sex marriage is really impossible because how do you decide on who is who when both was created with the same body parts, and who wears the dress and who wears the pants. Being that the Bible refers to the wedding gown of a woman numerous of times; someone is to wear the dress (Psalms 45-13). I never read in the Holy Bible where a man was wearing a wedding dress or any type of gown to a wedding. With the Bible also stating that men should not wear anything pertaining to a woman and vice versa, this backs up the same sex marriage confusion also (Deuteronomy 22:5). I'm for sure that many would say that you can dictate which person wears the dress or the pants by the way that they carry themselves. However, Jesus uses marriage as an example of his return for the church. He refers to the church as the bride and himself as the "Bridegroom" (Mark 2:19-20), (Ephesians 5:25-27). So even if a man was to misinterpret that scripture, he would still remain living his life abstaining from sex as a woman married to Jesus Christ would. Which means he would not live his life as a woman because his heart would not be darkened, neither will he be given over to vile passions or having sex with anyone. It's a good thing that Jesus has given the same sex or vile passion people a chance to

THE TOTALITY OF DELIVERANCE

change their ways because in earlier times they would stone them to death. (Leviticus 20:13) Just like a darkened heart vile passions also should be prayed and fast for, to be lifted up and removed from a person.

Reprobate Mind

Reprobate-(Noun) 1.) A depraved, unprincipled, or wicked person: a drunken reprobate.
2.) A person rejected by God and beyond hope of Salvation.

Mind- Is the set of cognitive faculties that enables consciousness, perception, thinking, judgment, and memory.

So, if we put the two words together according to both of its definitions; a reprobate mind would mean a wicked or rejected person by God, thoughts or way of thinking. When referring to homosexuality, the reprobate mind is when a person has a mind frame to say, father God in heaven I know that what I am doing is not your will for my life, as well as I know that it is completely wrong but I am going to do it anyway. This is one of the last things that the Holy Bible states, that God gives the Homosexuals over to because they know what a Godly relationship consist of. The Bible states, "And even as they did not like to retain God in their knowledge, God gave them over to a reprobate mind, to do those things which are not

THE TOTALITY OF DELIVERANCE

convenient (Romans 1:28)." They also know that the sexual desires are meant to be between a man and a woman because God has revealed it to them himself. He's revealed it many times and in many ways as well as writing it on their hearts. One of the most important facts has already been proven, being only a man and a woman can produce a child. This reprobate mind frame is the mind frame that no one should desire to have. It allows you to go forth with the despicable behavior of whatever you are doing, right along with rejecting Gods decision on it. In which, it makes him to say that, he's basically not dealing with you on this matter because of the choices that you are currently choosing to make. Also, God is saying that he's not even going to give you the mind frame to do right or even think right, since you are making the choice to intentionally disobey him. He is making it a well-known fact, that you are not one of his elects and your salvation is in dooms land at this current point of time in your life. It's very vital to retain God in our knowledge so that we can do the things that are convenient or better yet to live a life that is holy, pleasing and acceptable unto the almighty God. When coming out of a dark lifestyle like homosexuality, it is very important to keep your mind stayed on Jesus and the things above. You have to renew the spirit of your mind daily and most importantly you must stay away and refrain from "stinkin, thinkin."

THE TOTALITY OF DELIVERANCE

Meditating on the word day and night would be the best way to help yourself and God from giving you over to a reprobate mind. This mind set would cause you to live a sinful life and will not allow you to feel any remorse for the wrong things that you are doing or have done. A reprobate mind is a very dangerous mind set to have because, all of the traps that Satan has planned for your life, you will walk right into them willingly, without the mind frame to come out of them in a Godly manner. Being the mind is the battle field, you will be fighting on the wrong team in your mind on an everyday basis, until this mind set has been lifted from you. A great example of someone who is under this mindset would be a couple, that is of the same sex and have agreed upon marriage. Marriage is clearly spoken in the Bible over and over again between a man and a woman. The person under the reprobate mind is clearly aware that this is not in God's will for anyone's life but still persist to go deeper into this sinful way of living. In which if the person has a call on his life and then begins the deliverance process, it will only make it to be an even harder struggle to come out of homosexuality. Being how deeply rooted and grounded they were living in this sin nature or sinful way of life. Yet, there is still no sin that is too deep for God to bring you out of or save you from. It's just the pressure during the deliverance process that is extremely difficult, but one

THE TOTALITY OF DELIVERANCE

must consider their way or choice of lifestyle before this new way of living had begun. There will be many demons to fight off of you, on a daily basis, as well as many of temptations that Satan, is able to send your way because of the sinful nature that you had indulged in. It would be very important to pray for the mind of Christ to be in you as well as keeping your mind stayed on Jesus at all times. When overcoming a reprobate mind we must continue to renew our minds daily as well as pray for the renewing of the right spirit within us. Also, ask God to let the mind that was in Christ Jesus also be in you. This mindset would have to be lifted from you by God and God only. You would start by repenting, thinking differently, a change of heart and much, much prayer and fasting.

The Process

The process when you have made up your mind to come out of this lifestyle of darkness is a total challenge all by itself. There will be many of nights where you are lying awake all night, wondering how will I ever make it until tomorrow? There is much love lost for you, from your friends and family because their eyes are not open yet. They still have a darkened heart and fail to realize that you have been chosen by the living God of host, to be a representative of his kingdom living here on earth. The tears are like rivers of streaming waters, from the heart aches and the pain that must be flushed out of your system from past failures, disappointments and defeats in your life. You must forgive yourself from everything and everyone that has caused these confusions. Then move on, all the while you are using these confusions to help edify someone else's, life journey that is going through similar struggles. The sorrow from having to resist the urges that you once obeyed so well and agreed to in the past is mind boggling. The many of friends that you use to love so dear, that must be cut off in order for you to move forward in life. As you continue to grow in faith and from

THE TOTALITY OF DELIVERANCE

glory to glory and getting closer to God while adhering to the unction's of the Holy Spirit, the more uncomfortable the people you are around will become. When you really look around you, while you are in this process you will notice that you will be alone. God uses many of different ways, to teach us the things that we need to know during this point in our lives. Sometimes God will even allow you to go down the wrong road in life and allow the enemy to attack you, just so you can tell someone else not to go down that same road. There are many of things that God will not inform you on, that you will go through; that will leave you without understanding and wondering why did you have to go through this season of your life. God uses this measure to teach us faith in him and to trust, that if he brought you to it he will bring you through it. There was one thought, that was controversial in my mind and that was, now that I am a Christian, in spite of everything that I have been through, do I have to show love to everyone? In the sense where, most of my friends would disagree with this decision of the process for total deliverance, but God did not. We must put on love because God is love and has so much love for the world. Remember that, God so loved the world that he gave his only begotten son that who so ever believe in him should not perish but have eternal life (John 3:16). When we as sinners come to God we come looking for a new life, new

THE TOTALITY OF DELIVERANCE

mind set and love through Christ Jesus. With the mindset, that I want to be free from sin and my past shameful lifestyle and converted to a new presentable lifestyle that represents God. This means that you will be totally different from others who have not come to this new mindset yet, and still agrees with the nature of your past. The Holy Bible teaches us that, "If any man be in Christ he is a new creature: old things are passed away; behold, all things are become new (2Corinthians 5:17). From this scripture I learned that not only do I have to let go of my old way of thinking but I also have to let go of the events and people of my past. So if they don't want to show more love, they are missing the biggest part of God and are not thinking with the mind of Christ or walking in the newness of life. Now that we are saved, we should be under new leadership and a new way of thinking as well as belief through the Holy Spirit. In which, the bible teaches that people who are in the world and the people that are in God will not see eye to eye because, "it is the Holy Spirit who leads into all truth. The world cannot receive him, because it isn't looking for him. But you know him, because he lives with you now and later will be in you (John 14:17)." Although the majority of my friends and family have deserted me on this journey because we do not see eye to eye, it does not bother me, as much after I read that Jesus said himself, "No I will not abandon you as

THE TOTALITY OF DELIVERANCE

orphans-I will come to you (John 14:18). Which institutes that being alone does not consist of loneliness. "It's the peace of mind and heart, that Christ Jesus has left us as a gift that the world cannot give. So I'm not troubled or afraid (John 14:27)". Being we love him, accepts, and obey his commandments, you must refuse to allow anyone to conduct your way of life or let their outlook or input on your life stop you from Jesus Christ. Learning to observe the things of the Almighty God may not be all that easy but it is definitely well worth it in the end. We have got to keep it moving until we make it to our final destination! Heaven!

Praise and Worship

Praise-(Verb) Express warm approval or admiration of
  Synonyms: commend, applaud, eulogize, compliment, congratulate, lionize, admire, hail, ballyhoo laud

Worship- The feeling or expression of reverence and adoration for a deity.
  Synonyms: reverence, veneration, adoration, glory, exaltation, devotion, praise, thanksgiving, honor, magnification.

Praise and Worship should not just be done at church, for it is a Lifestyle or a way of life. Coming out of a lifestyle that is so demonic and so dark and gloomy according to God and his Holy word, we must make sure that we are continually praising and worshiping God, at all times. This should be the new lifestyle or way of life for the person that is being delivered. Knowing that we need God on a constant basis; praise and worship is what actually helps to keep us alive during and after the deliverance process. The Holy Bible informs us that God inhabits the praises of his people (Psalms 22:3). In which that means God lives in

THE TOTALITY OF DELIVERANCE

praise and whenever God is around there is a peaceful surrounding filled with his glory that is in-explainable. The atmosphere changes when God is around, demons must flee, healing is produced, your feelings and emotions begin to change for the good. Even if it is just a sporadic thought to remind ourselves that we must give God the praise, the glory and the honor, just be sure to always give God the praise. Be prepared to stop whatever you are doing to give God praise or begin to worship him when circumstances become to be a difficult task for you. Even if you are around many of people, find you a space of your own or maybe even a restroom to go and give God the Glory. I noticed that the enemy will cause things to happen around you, to get to your mind and to frustrate you by stealing your attention off of God and putting it on the situation. This type of attack would need to be handled as soon as possible, through immediate praise and worship. First reason is because we should not live or eat on milk (babies in Christ) for a very long time on this journey, but meat. Then, knowing that the enemy does not like our praise or our worship, this would be great weaponry to fight back with under this kind of attack. Sometimes we have to honor God for just being God all by himself and for the things that he has done. As well as the things that we are asking him to do with our lives now and for the future. This helps with letting God know that we are thankful to be called a child of the most, high God and validates that we are now living for his glory. Also, with constant praise in worship I personally believe that it reflects the God in us, and it allows Satan and his kingdom to know that we know who we are and whom we belong to. Praise and Worship is also a great defense against the kingdom of darkness, that either helps to stop spiritual warfare or help you to come through it. Dealing with spiritual warfare or (taking a stand against supernatural evil forces), we need to be also girded up in our full armor of God.

Girded up, with our full armor on, along with praise and worship, will allow us to remain standing during the unannounced battles of the enemy's most vicious tactics, against our lives. Praise and Worship can be done in many of ways. You don't have to necessarily jump, yell, or scream and shout, but you do want to get yourself into that mode of thinking, that is coming from the inside out. From my understanding, the Bible tells us that Satan was the minster of music around the throne of God before his great fall. In which, this signifies that God created, loves and enjoys to "HEAR" the praises and worship of his people. This is also extremely vital to the Deliverance process, because when we are being delivered we are giving ourselves over to the things of God and the things that God desires for us to do or be. Praise and Worship

THE TOTALITY OF DELIVERANCE

along with meditation is definitely a part of this transformation and shall be done at all times for the rest of our lives. Always take time out to praise and worship the God of our salvation!

Spiritually Walking

Spirit led must be spirit Fed. The Holy Bible teaches us that we are not just flesh but also spiritual beings and that we should walk in the spirit. That we would not, fulfill the lust of the flesh (Galatians 5:16-18). With God being a spirit, if we are always walking in the spirit we will be walking to the beat of God's drum. In which we would be walking according to God's voice. There would be no reason for a season of unawareness to anything, because God will order your steps by letting you know who, what, when and where you are in your life. The biggest distraction that you will face while walking in the spirit is your own human mind frame. We must continue to keep our minds stayed on Jesus and the cross as well as staying in constant prayer and fasting. With keeping our minds on the things above (kingdom thinking), it would leave little room for our minds to slip away to worldly things, (things of the flesh or carnal thinking). It also helps with keeping closed doors shut. In which if you are always in the spirit (Holy Spirit), you will be able to do the things of the spirit like hearing, seeing as well as fighting in the spirit instead of in the flesh. As the Holy Bible states, we are not fighting against

THE TOTALITY OF DELIVERANCE

flesh and blood but against the rulers, against the authorities, against the powers of this dark world and against the spiritual forces of evil in the heavenly or high places (Ephesians 6:12). The Holy Bible also informs us that our weapons are not carnal but spiritual and mighty to the bringing down of strong holds (2Corinthians 10:4). Notice, the scriptures gratifies the fact of how we are to use the things in the spirit to obtain what we need in order to survive this journey of war and battles of strong things. With strong holds being those things that either attract you or manipulate you to not let them go, even with you knowing that they are not God's will for your life. Fighting in the spirit will defeat these strong holds, for it is God who is doing the fighting for you. As you already know the bible tells us to sit still, until God make our enemies our foot stools (Luke 20:43). Be careful not to allow the strong holds to keep you in bondage for a long time because they will soon turn into things that we are holding strongly too.

With you beginning, to live or sow things in the spirit you will then begin to reap things in the spirit. Nevertheless, walking in the spirit will help you defeat any lifestyle or strong hold that tries to separate man from God. Allowing the Holy Spirit to lead you will remove the majority of your unnecessary stumbling blocks out of your way, during this Christian Journey. I believe that walking in the spirit is another way of life. You can allow the spirit to talk for you or give you the words to say (Luke 12:12). I am a witness to the spirit telling you what to do or say, as well as this book or literature that you are reading is also an example of the results from the spirit, speaking through me. The spirit knows the spirit. For who knows a person's thoughts except their own spirit within them? In the same way no one knows the thoughts of God except the Spirit of God (1Corinthians 2:11). Walking in the Holy Spirit of God would also help the Homosexuals to come to an understanding of what it is that God desires and requires for your life. It is almost impossible to come out of any dark lifestyle without walking with the Spirit of God leading you. There will come many of times where you will not know, what to do or how to handle certain situations. Being, this will be a new start for you, you will need to be taught new ways and the old ways that you had thought or was taught that was right, will need to be put behind you with your old lifestyle. The Holy Spirit will then begin to lead you and teach you the new way that God is trying to establish on your path to Holiness. This new journey that you are approaching will lead you to the path of righteousness and pure holiness. For without holiness no man will see God (Hebrews 12:14), in which this scripture is a witness that the life that we are living is meant to be holy and spirit lead. Also we need to pray in the spirit, so

THE TOTALITY OF DELIVERANCE

that when we are lost for words and do not know what to pray for, the spirit will pray for us and alert our inner man on which way we should go. The Holy Spirit will search our hearts and minds to find out what we need prayer for and deliver it to God on our behalf. Remember that God is a spirit and those who worship him must do it in spirit and in truth. (John 4:24)

Power From On High

Power- 1.) The ability to do something or act in a particular way, especially as a faculty or quality.
Synonyms: ability, capacity, capability, potential, faculty, competence

2.) The capacity or ability to direct or influence the behavior of others or the course of events.

We must obtain the power that comes from heaven in order to carry out the whole deliverance process. The power that Jesus had as well as more power, being he has risen and has gone back to the father. In the Holy Bible we first see the power of Jesus when he turned the water into wine. Then from there he made the dumb to talk, the lame to walk, the blind to see, he had power to cast demons out of other people, he even had the power to raise the dead. Jesus had the power to complete his journey and reach his final destination without falling for the temptations or fiery darts from Satan. In order to obtain full deliverance, it takes this power to keep you

THE TOTALITY OF DELIVERANCE

from falling or going back to where God has brought you from. With the ability to strongly say, "That when I am weak I am then strong." This power even allows you to turn down the offers that Satan, that cunning serpent sends out towards the believers of Christ. Jesus told his apostles that when he goes back to the father that they shall receive power after the Holy Spirit has come upon you (Acts1:8). He also told them to wait on it and once you receive it the Holy Spirit will teach you all things. I believe that it is safe enough to say that it is impossible to fulfill this walk or overcome the world without this power. You must be seriously certain that you are ready to walk in this power and to fulfill the destiny that God has set out and planned for your life. From the beginning of time God had already planned our lives to whom and what we are to become. Power from on high will help you change the things that are inside of you that you feel no one else here on earth can help with. The urges that make you want to do the things that are strong holds will also be under the command of this power. I truly believe that this is God himself giving us a little more of him to help us with the things that are far out of human reach. For in the model prayer that Jesus taught his disciples in the Holy Bible, ended with telling God that "he is the power" (Matthew 6:13). This Power of God that comes through his Holy Spirit will allow us to use the strength that comes by faith

THE TOTALITY OF DELIVERANCE

through Christ Jesus our Lord and savior. In which we will then be able to heal the sick, raise the dead and cause God's kingdom to be revealed on earth. Basically to perform the same miracles that king Jesus did when he was here walking the earth and more. When it comes to the Homosexuals, this power from on high will be mandatory. Being, the Holy Bible states that there are so many sins connected to this lifestyle, the temptation is extremely harsh at the beginning of the deliverance process; as well as Satan's tricks to make you stumble. You must use the power of God to shut this system down as it will be extremely challenging but this power is literally God doing the fighting for you; once you have called forth his reinforcements. We must pray hard and learn how to obtain and use this power throughout our daily lives, so that we will be able to persevere through a world so dark and perverse. Without this Power from on High or God's power the deliverance will not take place. In which, this suggests, that we must be filled with the Holy Spirit in order to receive this power. Pray for Power from on High.

THE TOTALITY OF DELIVERANCE

Perseverance

Persevere- To continue in a course of action even in the face of difficulty or with little or no prospect of success.

When overcoming a lifestyle such as homosexuality or any other demonic lifestyle, it takes much perseverance. As tough as it may be you must never stop or give up on your goal. This is a change in your life that must be pursued with your whole heart, mind, body, soul and spirit. It will be a complete total challenge to overcome this obstacle; because there are many strong holds and demonic forces that are behind the spirit of this lifestyle. You must go through every heart ache, every massive emotional state of the mind with much perseverance, in spite of how you really feel. The spirits are so dark that they not only, get inside of the person and change their appearance but it also changes their environment too. It also changes your way of life, so you must struggle with the complications that comes with coming out of this dark side, of your life. Once you feel like you have overcome the hardest part of it all, that's when it gets even harder. Satan and his team refuses to let go of the mind challenges or the temptation that he throws towards the over comers. Satan does not mind reminding you of your past as well as the continuous approach, on re-offering you a chance to rejoin the lifestyle again. In spite of the bad dreams, all of the discouragement, temptation at its best for your weakest desires, much, much, persecution as well as trying to condemn the person of their past, you must persevere through it all. Do not stop! You have immediately, became an open threat to the kingdom of darkness. With how hard you must pray and stay in contact with God to overcome this lifestyle, you will be full and filled with the Holy Spirit at all times. Which means you will be a constant witness to the Kingdom of God's, life changing testimony. As well as, the fruits of the spirit will began to be noticed in your life, because the spirit of the Lord will be upon you. The deliverance process to get to this new lifestyle will cause a lot of suffering and losses and the testing of your "Faith." In which Faith is the substance of things hope for and the evidence of things not seen (Hebrews 11:1). Faith is another key element in this deliverance process that you must really obtain and hold on to. Faith would really help with the perseverance process because it will help you to learn endurance. The bible teaches us that the testing of your Faith allows your endurance to grow. So let it grow, for when your endurance is fully developed, you will be perfect and complete, needing nothing (James 1:3-4).

THE TOTALITY OF DELIVERANCE

However, the Holy Bible teaches us to glory in our sufferings because we know that suffering produces perseverance and perseverance produces character and character brings hope. Hope does not put us to shame because God's love has been poured out into our hearts through the Holy Spirit who has been given to us (Romans 5:3-5). In order to really overcome the dark lifestyle of homosexuality, you must remember to persevere and press toward the mark for the prize of the high calling of God in Christ Jesus (Philippians 3:14). Although, sometimes your way may seem dark but we must be encouraged to see God. Sometimes you have to encourage yourself because there will be times when there will be no one around who understands what you are going through. We must also keep in mind that Jesus Christ has already overcome the world and the "Kingdom of Darkness" is definitely not a threat to God. In fact the Kingdom of Darkness is only a threat to our minds but continue to persevere through the good times and the bad times for your reward will be eternal life with Jesus Christ! Keep in mind that, the race is not given to the swift or to the strong but to the one that endures until the end (Ecclesiastes 9:11). Pray for strength to persevere through it all and our God who never sleeps nor slumber will always be there to strengthen you in your weakest hour. Pray for God's sweet peace, because it will help you with

THE TOTALITY OF DELIVERANCE

the perseverance, because of the calmness and relaxation it brings with its presence.

Set Free

When you are totally delivered, you are now considered set free from the, sins of your past, every chain that had you bound and every bad spirit that used to live inside of you. They all have been released! A new way of life has begun, because of Jesus Christ going to the cross and finishing what God his father, required him to do for the price of sin. In which God has totally redeemed your past life and set you free. However you are not exempt from making mistakes but if you are filled with the Holy Spirit and very sensitive to him, he will direct you in all manners of righteousness. You will not become a perfect person but you are to strive for perfection. Being the Holy Bible states, that we should be perfect because your heavenly father is perfect (Matthew 5:48). There is no one who is perfect but Jesus he is the only one capable of walking this earth with no sin. Even, with all that I have learned and the many of different teaching techniques that the Lord uses to train me, to be a better person; yet I am still not perfect. However, I try to be very cautious when it comes to making decisions in my life now. Mainly because, I have learned that wrong choices are the results for the majority

THE TOTALITY OF DELIVERANCE

of life's failures. If and when any temptation and different obstacles are presented to me, I begin to shut them down immediately. To make sure there are no open doors for the enemy to come in and cause havoc in my new life. I begin to seek direction from God, because I know that he has already made the way of escape in the time of temptation (1Corinthians 10:13). However there is not a time limit on how long it will take for your deliverance to actually come forth in its full entirety. Because it's ultimately Gods choice and decision on how long, when, and where your deliverance will take place. Also, it will depend on how deep into sin you were living, as well as your total obedience to God's instructions in your life. In the Holy Bible (Mark 5:1-18) there is a parable about Jesus going to the region of the Gerasenes. Where a man with an impure spirit approached Jesus, and as he fell to his knees the wicked spirit ask Jesus what did he want with him and told him that he was "Legion," because there were many of those spirits in that man. Jesus cast the spirits into a herd of pigs that all ran and drowned about 2000 of them. Jesus delivered the man but we do not know how long it took for the man to come through the deliverance process, because the scriptures do not report it. However it does report that the man had cut himself with rocks and ran around naked and could not be bound even with chains on, until Jesus had cast the impure spirits

THE TOTALITY OF DELIVERANCE

out of him. When the people who were watching seen this deliverance take place, they went and told the people of the city what Jesus had done, the people came back and saw the man clothed and in his right mind. Yet it still does not state how long it took to recover from the many of spirits that were in the man. The people then asked Jesus to leave their region, and as he began to get on the boat the man that he delivered asked to go with him. Of course Jesus told him to stay and go back to his family and tell them all the things that the Lord has done for him and the mercy that he had on him.

Once you are set free and living a lifestyle that is totally holy, acceptable and pleasing to God, you have become a witness of Gods Kingdom coming to earth. This means that your life is a testimony to the earth and everything that is in it. Revealing that the reason why Jesus Christ has come has paid off and is still working in this age of time. You are to begin to witness to the souls that are lost, help win souls for Christ, and help them that are in need of deliverance. Most of the time when God delivers someone from their past he is expecting you to tell others about the goodness of him and how he came into your life and changed it for the better. With the peace that Jesus Christ brings to your life being he is the 'Prince of Peace," you will be able to live a total life of great love, joy, peace and happiness. In which this kind of lifestyle, most humans

THE TOTALITY OF DELIVERANCE

long to be around. They also observe your life to find out what and how are you in such a peaceful state of mind, living in a world so dark and corrupted. This will allow you to be a living witness as well as the opportunity to spread the good news of the gospel of Jesus Christ to that person and many others. Knowing, discipleship is what we are called to do as Christians; pay very close attention to your surroundings, places and people that you come in contact with, because someone is always watching and paying attention to your actions. Being, we are to be beacons of light and salt to a dark and bitter world; do not allow anyone to challenge your Faith or your trust in Gods Holy Word. They will be sent to come and tell you that the Bible is not true, and neither is Jesus. Just let them know that it's not a debate, not only because the Bible is true and that Jesus did come and die and has risen, but because he now lives inside of you. They will be sent to discourage you from the truth which is Jesus Christ because without Jesus Christ, Satan knows that there will be no liberty at all. Apart from God we can do nothing (John 15:5). Do not worry or be afraid of anything, just pray to have the mind of Christ and it will help you to stay in great Faith. Keep this scripture in mind at all times. For I am persuaded, that neither death, nor life, nor angels, nor principalities, nor powers, nor things present, nor things to come, nor height, nor depth, nor any other creature, shall be able to

THE TOTALITY OF DELIVERANCE

separate us from the love of God, which is in Christ Jesus our Lord. (Romans 8:38-39)

Your New Character

Finding out your new character and personality will be another one of the most challenging hurdles in this entire deliverance process. Depending upon how long you were portraying and living the character that you are trying to change from; will play a major part of the time change in your personalities and your new character. Being your character is not just an overnight creation but is the outcome of a number of things like: people, places, thoughts, plans, teachings, education, family traits, family curses, and your personal beliefs, etc. Now that you are becoming a new person you must take the time out to really search the things that are going to help shape out your new character. When it comes to the homosexuals that are feminine, they would have to find masculine men to watch and scope out some of their everyday moves. Specifically men of God, and heterosexual men, that carry themselves with much integrity that can have a big influence upon your life. You must be serious about becoming a new character because your old nature, have ways and mannerisms that are embedded in your current personality and is in the need of change. You also must

THE TOTALITY OF DELIVERANCE

open up and allow the Holy Spirit to show you and teach you how a true man of God should carry himself. Do not become offended with the different types of measures that the Holy Spirit will use to reveal Godly ways to you, or things that he wants you to change. Some examples are: internet and its different sites, television, different people, friends, family members and many other things that you would not expect. You also must want to feel like a man of wholeness in order to change your personality and to receive a new character. Pay very close attention to how men carry themselves when they are out in public and when they are just around every day normal friends and family members. Listen to the words that they say and the different paraphrases that they use to communicate with others. Even watch their body gestures, in which it would be less movement than a feminine homosexual. The reason for this is because the homosexual guys have many of spirits that gets inside of you and change you from the inside out. Most people could recognize the homosexual spirit almost a mile away if a person has lived as a feminine guy for a while. To be honest there are some feminine guys that are straight but because they are not homosexuals I would just consider them soft men or men that are not as aggressive as others (Softy's). Unfortunately those spirits in the homosexual would accuse almost every man of being a homosexual, specially

THE TOTALITY OF DELIVERANCE

the soft men, but this is not true. With that being said it's ok to be on this Christian journey and not have come in total contact with your masculine side at first, because it's your inside that God wants and he will do the work on the rest.

This part of the deliverance process will most likely take the longest to recover from, if you are feminine. Be careful not to let the enemy tell you that you are not delivered or in the process of changing because of the femininity that others may still see in you. This is just another one of Satan's tricks to try to knock you off of course and discouragement. You must remember that this deliverance is a process and for some people it will take many of years to come through this process. I believe it takes double the time that you lived in your last character to develop your new character. So for an example, if your character for ten years was feminine I believe it will take twenty years to fully develop your new masculine characteristics. This is the time where metamorphosis will take its course in your life physically. The law of attraction says that "the way a person carries themselves will attract others of the same countenance." In contrast, this femininity could sometimes be used as a camouflage to attract souls to win for Christ, which was my personal experience.

THE TOTALITY OF DELIVERANCE

Remember to love yourself. Most of all put on Christ and wear him around and you will be treated in the same manner as Jesus. Jesus entire message in the Holy Bible encourages all believers to change, turning from our wicked ways regardless of your choice of sin.

Knowing that living in the homosexual lifestyle; most of our characteristics are not of a man of God. We must put on a new character that portrays the God in us. The Holy Bible states, "Therefore If any man be in Christ, he is a new creature: old things are passed away; behold, all things are become new."(2Corinthians 5:17)

THE TOTALITY OF DELIVERANCE

My Outlook On Total Deliverance

As I begun this life changing process, I noticed that getting into a relationship with someone does not define the person that you really are inside. Just because you are a male in a relationship with a female does not mean that you are delivered from the spirit of confusion or the homosexuality spirit. Often times, most people mistaken the changing of sex's in your spouse selection with being delivered. This is what causes the total confusion with heterosexual relationships. When one of the partners has not been delivered from that spirit of the same sex, mind set yet. In which this is a very deep dark spirit that only God can deliver you from. Depending on how deep you indulged into this lifestyle before you walked towards the deliverance process, will determine the healing and delivering process timing. Sometimes people get delivered instantly others have to go through an, over the time process because of how deeply rooted and grounded that you were into the beliefs of this lifestyle or your way of life. Being our battlefield is of the mind a person dealing with this spirit, that has lived most of their life in this lifestyle would have to retrain their thinking process as well as their outlook and input on life. Now that you have

THE TOTALITY OF DELIVERANCE

begun this process, you must obtain wisdom, knowledge and understanding from God. Being that he ultimately is the one who designed all human kind and set the rules to this life that we are living. As for me this was a process that God had to take me step by step and piece by piece showing me what's the good and the bad in everything that I had once believed in or on. Once you have been totally delivered you will know it just by looking at yourself in the mirror and the people that are around you will know it as well. Most of the time, when the homosexual spirit enters into a human, it begins to change the body into another form; which allows this spirit to be picked up by other familiar spirits to alert them that this is one of their "kind." When you realize this change in yourself, you will also recognize that your body puts off a new aura that most of your family and friends will see or sense. Once God has delivered you from this lifestyle you must never indulge in any part of it again. Being that the kingdom of darkness will already be on alert that you have been delivered and Satan will send many offers your way to reel you back in. You must stay in constant prayer and fasting, as well as living a lifestyle that is completely holy and acceptable unto God or the total deliverance will not last. I have noticed that the unction of the Holy Spirit is the most important factor and key to surviving this Journey. This is a Christian journey that transforms your mind and requires

THE TOTALITY OF DELIVERANCE

a daily dosage of the word of God. Most people would say, that it does not take all of that but I see different. The moment I take my mind off of Jesus that is the moment that my mind begins to fall back into the old way of thinking. In which it is our thought process that also holds the key to temptation. In order to keep my mind stayed on Jesus I have to keep praising and singing songs in my head. This kind of praising and song singing is not done with the mouth but is done with your Spirit. It is the spirit of a man that God is after, not necessarily the physical part of you. In which, God is a spirit so everyone that worships him must do it in spirit and in truth. I would suggest you to watch out for serpents that are sent your way to distract you from completing this life long journey. Satan is going to use some of his most cunning tricks on you. The majority of those tricks, once you have gotten this far in the deliverance process, will appear to be beacons of Light. Or so called saints, but really and truly they are of the kingdom of darkness and have come to only knock you off of your journey with Jesus Christ. They will tell you all kinds of things to confuse you to mess up your way of thinking.

Being most things begin with a thought including temptation, it is extremely vital to remain walking in the spirit so that you can recognize a wrong or contrary spirit. In conclusion be aware at all times and pray for God to

THE TOTALITY OF DELIVERANCE

give you the discernment that is required to complete this Christian Race.

THE TOTALITY OF DELIVERANCE

(Romans 1:18-32)

[18] The wrath of God is being revealed from heaven against all the godlessness and wickedness of people, who suppress the truth by their wickedness, [19] since what may be known about God is plain to them, because God has made it plain to them. [20] For since the creation of the world God's invisible qualities—his eternal power and divine nature—have been clearly seen, being understood from what has been made, so that people are without excuse.

[21] For although they knew God, they neither glorified him as God nor gave thanks to him, but their thinking became futile and their foolish hearts were darkened. [22] Although they claimed to be wise, they became fools [23] and exchanged the glory of the immortal God for images made to look like a mortal human being and birds and animals and reptiles.

[24] Therefore God gave them over in the sinful desires of their hearts to sexual impurity for the degrading of their bodies with one another. [25] They exchanged the truth about God for a lie, and worshiped and served created things rather than the Creator—who is forever praised. Amen.

[26] Because of this, God gave them over to shameful

lusts. Even their women exchanged natural sexual relations for unnatural ones. ²⁷ In the same way the men also abandoned natural relations with women and were inflamed with lust for one another. Men committed shameful acts with other men, and received in themselves the due penalty for their error.

²⁸ Furthermore, just as they did not think it worthwhile to retain the knowledge of God, so God gave them over to a depraved mind, so that they do what ought not to be done. ²⁹ They have become filled with every kind of wickedness, evil, greed and depravity. They are full of envy, murder, strife, deceit and malice. They are gossips, ³⁰ slanderers, God-haters, insolent, arrogant and boastful; they invent ways of doing evil; they disobey their parents; ³¹ they have no understanding, no fidelity, no love, no mercy. ³² Although they know God's righteous decree that those who do such things deserve death, they not only continue to do these very things but also approve of those who practice them.

Acknowledgments

I must say that The Totality of Deliverance is a result of numerous hours of studying and seeking God for the proper directions for my life. That brought me to this walk of Faith in Christ Jesus, which then led me to an extreme compassion to help win souls and lead others to Christ.

I must show my love, my appreciation and my gratitude to my heavenly father, my Lord and Savior Jesus the Christ, my Holy Spirit. For all you have done for me. Words could never express the honor that I really feel about our God and him choosing this book to supernaturally reveal his image on. I thank you for the angels that you sent to inform me of things that I left out of the book and more things to put in it! Lord let this book carry out its job and course for its reason of creation and existence!

To my mother Janice Smith thank you for your inspiration, your wisdom, believing in me, and never giving up on me. Thanks for the long hours of listening and helping with the decision making for this book! I Love you dearly.

Tammy Taylor I thank you for all of your support and encouragement for this book and helping me to distribute the books thanks for believing in me and the ministry that

THE TOTALITY OF DELIVERANCE

God has placed inside of me! I love you!

Tykisha Pittman, I could have not achieved this book without your outstanding help. You are such a genius! I love you, thank you for believing in me and all you have done!

Desmond Owens, Anthony Hinton I thank you for being such an awesome help with the photos for this book and for taking the time out of your busy schedule to attend the photo shoots. Thanks for believing in me! I love you!

To Bishop Lambert Gates Sr. Thanks for being my spiritual father encouragement, edification, and welcoming me in with open arms and the opportunity to share my experience with Christ at Mt. Zion Apostolic church. I Love you!

Pastor Anita Stone, Minister Simpson(Scooter) thank you for accepting me with open arms and believing in me and the ministry that God has placed inside of me. Thanks for the inspiration and encouragement! I love you!

I would like to thank everyone that believes in me and have encouraged me to write this book. I love you all!

About The Author

Antwan Amey is a Christian believer who is on the team of winning souls for Jesus Christ. He was chosen by God and chooses to live his life totally for kingdom purposes only. At twenty-seven years of age the Lord would send Antwan into the world of ministry by ministering to every soul that God sends his way. Rather it is by his aura, his apparel, his worship, or ministering by mouth.

Through the life changing experience and his new journey with Jesus Christ, will help him to win the souls of not only his family but an unknown world. One by one and soul by soul! Antwan resides in the mid-western region of the United States of America. Delivered from the dark lifestyle of Homosexuality! In return he would help others that are dealing with the same lifestyle or any dark life style that is in need of deliverance and direction to Christ. Antwan is a first time author that plans to publish many helpful books, written under the unction of the Holy Spirit, to transform people lives and to win souls all over the world.

THE TOTALITY OF DELIVERANCE

Contact Info:

Apostle ForChrist AntwanAmey@Facebook

www.ameyantwan@yahoo.com

www.ameyantwanwordpress.com

Linkedin- Antwan Amey

THE TOTALITY OF DELIVERANCE

About the Editor

Stephanie Coleman is more than just the editor for my book but also a very close cousin that I hold very close and deep in my heart. Stephanie is a God fearing woman, loving wife and mother while she holds a very peculiar career of being an early child hood educator. She is wonderful with kids, as she teaches them and preps them to take on a big world with much intelligence and skills for success.

    Stephanie has always been one of my favorite cousins that I always loved to go and spend nights with her, and play as kids and even early teenage years as well. We carried similar traits and dreams as growing young adults. She has so much wisdom and is knowledgeable about so many things that it is well known outwardly. So much that when I told a few of my family members that she was editing my book this is what the response was:

Tykisha Pittman our cousin said, "Yes you picked the right person Stephanie is a Genius!"

THE TOTALITY OF DELIVERANCE

Tammy Taylor her sister said, "O it's going to be on point you know Stephanie is going to take her time and do it right!"

Janice Smith my mother said, "You know Stephanie is a school teacher and has been for years now, she will be the best person to do it!"

I didn't know who I was going to get to do it but the Lord God led me right to you and it was for a reason. I must tell you Stephanie thank you so much for everything that you have done to make this book possible. Including taking the time out of your extremely busy schedule to make sure it was the best of the best. I love you and I cannot express the appreciation I feel for your abundance of love and care that you have shown me and my book. May God continue to Bless you as you continue to be a blessing and not only to me but everyone that comes into contact with you. You are awesome! Thanks so much! You help make dreams come true!